olive

100 of the very best
CAKES AND BAKES

olive

100 of the very best
CAKES AND BAKES

olive *magazine*

The right of Immediate Media Company to be identified as
the author of this work has been asserted in accordance with the
Copyright, Designs and Patents Act 1988.

This edition first published in Great Britain in 2016 by
Orion, an imprint of the Orion Publishing Group Ltd
Carmelite House
50 Victoria Embankment
London, EC4Y 0DZ
An Hachette UK Company

10 9 8 7 6 5 4 3 2 1

A CIP catalogue record for this book is available
from the British Library.

ISBN: 978 1 4091 6224 7

Designed by Goldust Design

Printed in China

The Orion Publishing Group's policy is to use papers that are natural, renewable and recyclable
and made from wood grown in sustainable forests. The logging and manufacturing processes
are expected to conform to the environmental regulations of the country of origin.

Every effort has been made to fulfil requirements with regard to reproducing copyright material.
The author and publisher will be glad to rectify any omissions at the earliest opportunity.

www.orionbooks.co.uk

For more recipes visit olivemagazine.com

Contents

Introduction

olive is Britain's brightest food magazine. More than just a collection of recipes, it's about sharing the good stuff; cooking for family and friends, discovering great restaurants and enjoying weekends away. Upmarket and glossy, our recipe photography is the best in the market. In print and online at olivemagazine.com, we keep our audience up to date with new food trends and provide imaginative recipes for weeknights and weekends.

No matter the time of day or year, there is usually nothing a chocolatey biscuit or sticky lemon cake can't cure. In *100 of the Very Best Cakes and Bakes*, we put together a collection of our best cookie, cupcake, show-off cake and other bake recipes. Every recipe includes our trademark photography, so you know exactly what you are aiming for. From a simple sponge to a sloe gin layer cake, this is the only baking book you will need.

At **olive**, we believe you can still bake at home even if you don't have bags of time. Most of the recipes in this book can be made using easily accessible ingredients and equipment found in your kitchen. We think weekends are for more adventurous baking so we have also included some recipes that will take more time, but will be oh so worth it.

Notes and conversion tables

There are three categories of recipes throughout the **olive** books.

Easy: Most of our recipes come under this category and are very simple to put together with easy-to-find ingredients.
A little effort: These recipes require either more time, shopping for harder-to-find ingredients or a little more complicated cooking techniques.
Tricky but worth it: We have offered a few recipes that fall under this category and require a higher level of skill and concentration. These recipes give readers an occasional challenge but the little extra effort is always well worth the reward.

- Recipe timings are based on the total amount of time needed to finish the recipe so includes both prep and cook time.
- Provenance matters to us. Where possible, we use free-range eggs and chickens, humanely reared meat, organic dairy products, sustainably caught fish, unrefined sugar and fairly traded ingredients.
- Nutritional information is provided for all recipes. Because *olive* recipes don't always give exact quantities for ingredients such as oil and butter, nutritional quantities may not always be 100 per cent accurate. Analysis includes only the listed ingredients, not optional ingredients, such as salt, or any serving suggestions.
- Care should be taken when buying meat that you intend to eat raw or rare.
- Our recipes use large eggs, unless otherwise stated. Pregnant women, the elderly, babies and toddlers, and people who are unwell should avoid eating raw and partially cooked eggs.
- Vegetarians should always check the labels on shop-bought ingredients such as yogurt, cheese, pesto and curry sauces, to ensure they are suitable for vegetarian consumption.
- Unless otherwise specified, if oil is listed as an ingredient, any flavourless oil such as groundnut, vegetable or sunflower oil can be used.

Liquid measurements			
Metric	Imperial	Australian	US
25ml	1fl oz		
60ml	2fl oz	¼ cup	¼ cup
75ml	3fl oz		
100ml	3½fl oz		
120ml	4fl oz	½ cup	½ cup
150ml	5fl oz		
180ml	6fl oz	¾ cup	¾ cup
200ml	7fl oz		
250ml	9fl oz	1 cup	1 cup
300ml	10½fl oz	1¼ cups	1¼ cups
350ml	12½fl oz	1½ cups	1½ cups
400ml	14fl oz	1¾ cups	1¾ cups
450ml	16fl oz	2 cups	2 cups
600ml	1 pint	2½ cups	2½ cups
750ml	1¼ pints	3 cups	3 cups
900ml	1½ pints	3½ cups	3½ cups
1 litre	1¾ pints	1 quart or 4 cups	1 quart or 4 cups
1.2 litres	2 pints		
1.4 litres	2½ pints		
1.5 litres	2¾ pints		
1.7 litres	3 pints		
2 litres	3½ pints		

Oven temperature guide				
	Electricity			Gas
	°C	°F	(fan) °C	Mark
Very cool	110	225	90	¼
	120	250	100	½
Cool	140	275	120	1
	150	300	130	2
Moderate	160	325	140	3
	170	350	160	4½
Moderately hot	190	375	170	5
	200	400	180	6
Hot	220	425	200	7
	230	450	210	8
Very hot	240	475	220	9

Biscuits and tray bakes

Double-dipped peanut biscuits

1 hour, plus setting | makes 24 | easy

110g golden caster sugar
250g crunchy peanut
   butter
1 egg
100g dark chocolate,
   chopped
100g white chocolate,
   chopped

These biscuits are perfect for lovers of peanut butter and chocolate combinations.

Heat the oven to 170°C/Fan 150°C/Gas 4½ and line a couple of baking sheets with non-stick baking paper. Mix the sugar with the peanut butter and egg until it is thoroughly combined.

Divide the mixture into 24 even balls and place them on the baking sheets, about 5cm apart. Press them down gently so that they are of a uniform thickness. Bake for 35 minutes, or until lightly golden – don't over bake them or they'll get too hard. Transfer them to a wire rack and leave to cool completely.

Melt the chocolate in two separate bowls – set a heatproof bowl over a pan of simmering water, making sure the base of the bowl does not touch the water, or pop it in the microwave. Dip a half of each cooled biscuit in the dark chocolate then set aside on a piece of baking paper and leave to set completely. Once cooled, dip each biscuit in the white chocolate halfway up the dark chocolate. Leave to set as before.

Per biscuit 132 kcals, **protein** 3.6g, **carbohydrate** 9.7g, **fat** 8.7g, **saturated fat** 3.2g, **fibre** 0.5g, **salt** 0.1g

Pistachio and fig cookies

1 hour | makes about 40 cookies | easy

225g unsalted butter, softened

225g golden caster sugar

2 medium eggs

½ tsp vanilla extract

375g plain flour, plus extra for dusting

1 tsp baking powder

pinch of salt

150g pistachios, finely chopped

For the filling

200g ready-to-eat dried figs

juice and finely grated zest of 1 orange

1 tbsp clear honey

1 tbsp water

Think of these as a very sophisticated fig roll. These crumbly cookies keep really well in an airtight box for up to one week.

To make the filling, trim and discard the tough stalk from the figs and roughly chop the fruits. Put the figs in a pan with the orange juice and zest, honey and the water. Half cover the pan and set it over a low heat. Cook gently, stirring from time to time, until the figs are soft, adding more water if needed. Cool slightly then tip the mixture into a food processor and pulse briefly to break down any chunkier pieces.

To make the cookie dough, cream the butter and sugar until pale and light. Gradually beat in 1 whole egg and 1 egg yolk (keep the egg white, as you'll need it later) until smooth and combined. Mix in the vanilla extract. Sift the flour, baking powder and salt into the bowl, add 50g of the chopped pistachios and mix again until the dough comes together into a ball. Turn the dough out onto the work surface, divide it into 2 balls and flatten each into a disc. Cover with cling film and chill for 1 hour or until firm.

Dust the work surface with plain flour, roll a disc at a time into a 40 x 30cm rectangle roughly 2–3mm thick, then trim the edges. Spread half of the fig mix over the surface of the dough and scatter with 25g of the pistachios. With a long side nearest to you, roll the dough up into a tight cylinder, encasing the fig and pistachio mixture as you do so. Make sure the roll is tight, even, and not filled with air pockets. Wrap the roll in cling film and chill either in the fridge for 1 hour or the freezer for 30 minutes, until firm.

Repeat with the remaining dough, figs and another 25g of the pistachios. Heat the oven to 180°C/Fan 160°C/Gas 4. Unwrap the dough and brush with the reserved egg white. Roll the logs in the remaining 50g of pistachios to coat, and cut each log into 1cm thick slices. Arrange on lined baking sheets, leaving plenty of space in between each cookie, and bake in batches for 20 minutes or until golden and crisp. Cool on wire racks.

Per cookie 132 kcals, **protein** 2.2g, **carbohydrate** 16g, **fat** 6.7g, **saturated fat** 3.2g, **fibre** 1.3g, **salt** 0.1g

Soft-baked white chocolate and macadamia cookies

45 minutes | makes 30 large cookies | easy

225g unsalted butter,
  softened
200g light muscovado
  sugar
1 tsp vanilla extract
2 eggs, beaten
300g plain flour
1 tsp bicarbonate of soda
pinch of salt
75g dessicated coconut
250g white chocolate,
  chopped
150g macadamia nuts,
  chopped

Rich, buttery macadamia nuts make these cookies very indulgent.

Heat the oven to 180°C/Fan 160°C/Gas 4. Line two baking sheets with non-stick baking paper.

Cream the butter and sugar with an electric whisk until light and fluffy. Combine the vanilla and eggs and add them to the butter and sugar. Sift the flour, bicarbonate of soda and pinch of salt into the butter mix and fold in. Stir in the coconut, chocolate and nuts to evenly distribute them through the dough.

Drop rounded tablespoonfuls of the mixture onto the baking sheets, leaving about 4cm in between each cookie. Bake for about 10–15 minutes until golden brown, then leave to cool on the baking sheets – you might need to do this in batches. Once cool, store the cookies in an airtight box.

Per cookie 218 kcals, **protein** 2.7g **carbohydrate** 19.9g, **fat** 14.7g, **saturated fat** 6.9g, **fibre** 0.9g, **salt** 0.16g

Black and white pinwheel cookies

1 hour | makes about 40 cookies | easy

200g unsalted butter, at
  room temperature
150g golden caster sugar
2 tsp vanilla extract
1 egg
300g plain flour, sifted
25g cocoa powder

These cookies are delicious by themselves or served with ice cream or chocolate mousse. You can even make extra and keep them in the freezer.

Cream the butter and sugar using an electric mixer or a hand-held electric beater. Beat in the vanilla and egg, then add the flour. Beat until smooth then remove half the mixture and transfer it to another bowl. Beat the cocoa into half of the mixture. Shape both dough portions into rough oblongs then wrap in cling film and chill for 30 minutes until firm.

Roll out each lump of dough to a thickness of a £1 coin, trying to keep the oblong shape. Put the chocolate dough on top of the white dough and trim the edges to neaten. Roll up the two together, lengthways like a Swiss roll, then wrap in cling film and chill for 45 minutes.

Heat the oven to 180°C/Fan 160°C/Gas 4. Slice the dough into discs as thinly as you can, put them on a baking sheet lined with non-stick baking paper, spaced about 5cm apart, and cook for 15 minutes. Cool on wire racks.

Per cookie 83 kcals, **protein** 0.9g, **carbohydrate** 10.3g, **fat** 4.6g, **saturated fat** 2.7g, **fibre** 0.3g, **salt** 0.01g

Chocolate cherry cookies

30 minutes, plus chilling | makes 25 cookies | easy

225g dark chocolate,
  chopped
125g unsalted butter,
  softened
200g soft light brown sugar
2 eggs, beaten
1 tsp vanilla extract
150g plain flour
2 tsp baking powder
pinch of salt
100g desiccated coconut
150g natural coloured
  glacé cherries, washed,
  dried and chopped
2 tbsp whole milk
6 tbsp icing sugar

These cookies are inspired by the Australian Cherry Ripe chocolate bar – chewy coconut and glacé cherries covered in dark chocolate. Here you'll find the same flavours, just in cookie form.

Melt the chocolate in a heatproof bowl set over a pan of simmering water, making sure the base of the bowl does not touch the water, or in the microwave.

Cream the butter and soft light brown sugar together in a large mixing bowl until pale and light. Gradually add the beaten eggs, mixing well in between each addition, and then add the vanilla extract. Stir in the melted chocolate and mix until smooth. Sift the flour, baking powder and a pinch of salt over the mixture. Stir in the coconut, cherries and milk to evenly combine. Cover the bowl and chill for 2 hours or until firm.

Heat the oven to 180°C/Fan 160°C/Gas 4. Line two baking sheets with non-stick baking paper and tip the icing sugar into a bowl.

Scoop a heaped teaspoon of the cookie dough into the palm of your hand and roll it into a smooth ball roughly the size of a small walnut. Roll the cookie in the icing sugar to coat it thickly and put it on the baking sheet. Repeat with the remaining cookie dough, keeping the cookies spaced well apart. Bake in batches on the middle shelf of the oven for about 12 minutes until the tops are firm but not crisp. Leave the cookies to cool on the baking sheets.

Per cookie 191 kcals, **protein** 2g, **carbohydrate** 25g, **fat** 10g, **saturated fat** 6g, **fibre** 1g, **salt** 0.2g

Pistachio and passion fruit yo-yos

1 hour, plus cooling | makes 20 biscuits | easy

175g unsalted butter, softened
75g icing sugar, sifted
2 tbsp passion fruit juice, sieved
225g plain flour
½ tsp baking powder
50g cornflour
pinch of salt
25g unshelled unsalted pistachios, finely chopped

For the filling
100g white chocolate, chopped
75g unsalted butter, softened
150g icing sugar
2 passion fruit

These melt-in-the-mouth little sandwiched biscuits are a classic Australian tea-time bake. Pistachio and passion fruit make a sweet and welcome summertime treat.

Heat the oven to 160°C/Fan 140°C/Gas 3 and line 2 baking sheets with non-stick baking paper.

Make the cookies first. Cream the butter and icing sugar with electric beaters until very pale and light. Add the passion fruit juice and mix well. Sift the plain flour, baking powder, cornflour and a pinch of salt into the bowl, add the chopped pistachios and mix well. You will find it easier to use your hands to bring the dough together into a smooth, neat ball.

Break off large, cherry-sized nuggets of dough, roll them into smooth balls and arrange them on the prepared baking sheets. You should have 40 even-sized balls. Firmly press the tines of a fork into the top of each cookie to flatten them slightly and bake the cookies on the middle shelf of the oven for about 12–14 minutes until pale golden brown. Leave to cool on the baking sheet.

To make the filling, melt the chocolate in a heatproof bowl set over a pan of simmering water, making sure the base of the bowl does not touch the water, or in the microwave. Stir until smooth and leave to cool slightly.

Cream the butter and icing sugar until smooth, pale and light. Add the passion fruit and melted white chocolate and beat until smooth and spreadable. Spread the underside of half of the yo-yo cookies with a teaspoon of filling and sandwich with the remaining cookies.

Per biscuit 209 kcals, **protein** 1.8g, **carbohydrates** 23.8g, **fat** 12g, **saturated fat** 7.2g, **fibre** 0.7g, **salt** 0.1g

Chocolate and jasmine tea kisses

1 hour | makes 14 | easy

250g butter, very soft
50g icing sugar
250g plain flour
50g custard powder
1 tsp jasmine tea leaves,
  finely crushed

For the jasmine filling
1 jasmine tea bag
2 tbsp boiling water
100g butter
200g icing sugar
50g 72% dark chocolate,
  melted
50g good-quality milk
  chocolate, melted

These little cakes make a beautiful tea-time treat or afternoon snack. The half-dipped chocolate feels indulgent but does not overpower the delicate, aromatic flavour of the jasmine tea.

Heat the oven to 190°C/Fan 170°C/Gas 5. Line one or two baking sheets with non-stick baking paper. Put the butter, sugar, flour, custard powder and tea leaves in a processor and whizz to a soft dough.

Spoon the dough into a piping bag fitted with a round nozzle. Pipe 28 small round biscuits on the baking sheets and press down on each with a wet finger to get rid of any peaks. Bake for 15–20 minutes or until firm to the touch. Leave to cool completely.

For the filling, put the tea bag in a small jug and pour over 2 tablespoons of boiling water. Leave to steep for 10 minutes. Meanwhile, beat the butter and sugar together until light and creamy. Squeeze out the teabag to get the maximum flavour of the tea, then pour the water into the butter and sugar and beat to combine.

Sandwich two biscuits together with a little of the filling. Mix the two melted chocolates together then dip half of each biscuit sandwich in the chocolate and leave to set on a sheet of baking paper. Repeat with all the biscuits.

Per biscuit 369 kcals, **protein** 2.3g, **carbohydrate** 37g, **fat** 23.3g, **saturated fat** 14.5g, **fibre** 1.1g, **salt** 0.4g

Blackberry ripple ice cream sandwiches

40 minutes, plus freezing | makes 12 | easy

125g butter

100g light muscovado sugar

3 tbsp golden syrup

300g plain flour

1 tsp bicarbonate of soda

2 tsp ground ginger

For the no-churn ice cream

200g blackberries

2 tbsp caster sugar

600ml double cream

200ml condensed milk

1 tsp vanilla extract

The coolest, most irresistible ice cream sandwiches in existence. They're surprisingly quick to make and the ice cream requires no churning whatsoever!

Heat the oven to 200°C/Fan 180°C/Gas 6. To make the gingerbread, melt the butter, sugar and syrup in a pan. Put the flour, bicarb and ginger in a bowl and gradually mix in the melted ingredients to make a dough.

Divide the dough in half, then roll each piece out in between two sheets of baking paper to approximately 5mm thick. Put the pieces on separate baking sheets lined with non-stick baking paper and bake for 10–12 minutes, then take out and cool a little.

Take a 28 x 18cm (approximately) brownie tin and line it with a double sheet of cling film. While they are still warm, trim the two pieces of gingerbread so that they will fit inside the tin.

To make the ice cream, put the berries and sugar in a pan and heat, stirring until the sugar melts and the fruit breaks down, then push the mixture through a sieve to make a seedless sauce. Put the cream, condensed milk and vanilla in a bowl and beat with electric beaters until softly whipped.

Put a piece of the gingerbread in the bottom of the lined tin. Spoon the ice cream mix on top, then spoon over the berry sauce and gently ripple it through using a spoon. Top with the other piece of gingerbread and freeze overnight. Cut into squares to serve.

Per sandwich 540 kcals, **protein** 5g, **carbohydrate** 44.7g, **fat** 37.5g, **saturated fat** 23.2g, **fibre** 1.7g, **salt** 0.5g

Raspberry and lemon flapjacks

45 minutes, plus cooling | makes 12 | easy

75g butter
125g soft brown sugar
2 tbsp golden syrup
250g porridge oats
30g flaked almonds
zest and juice of 3 lemons
3 eggs
200g golden caster sugar
3 tbsp plain flour
100g raspberries
icing sugar, to dust

Flapjacks make the best after-school or mid-afternoon treat. With a delicious layer of raspberries, these oat bars are sure to be a hit with friends and family.

Heat the oven to 180°C/Fan 160°C/Gas 4. Gently melt the butter, brown sugar and golden syrup together and stir in the oats, almonds and a pinch of the lemon zest. Tip the mixture into a 24 x 19cm baking tin that is greased and lined with non-stick baking paper. Pack the oat mix into the bottom of the tin using the back of a spoon. Bake for 30 minutes, or until the base is set and crisp. Take the tin out of the oven and leave to cool while you make the topping.

Mix together the remaining lemon zest, the eggs and caster sugar, then stir in the flour and finally the lemon juice and beat until smooth. Pour this carefully over the flapjack base and drop the raspberries all over it at intervals. Bake for a further 15 minutes, or until the top of the mixture has set, then leave to cool completely in the tin before cutting the flapjack into bars. Dust with icing sugar to serve.

Per bar 317 kcals, **protein** 6.5g, **carbohydrate** 42.4g, **fat** 12.9g, **saturated fat** 6.2g, **fibre** 2.7g, **salt** 0.2g

Toasted almond and caramel millionaires' shortbread

1 hour, plus cooling | makes 16 | a little effort

200g butter, very cold, plus
  extra for greasing
100g plain flour
85g blanched almonds,
  toasted and finely
  chopped
25g rice flour
60g light muscovado sugar
pinch of salt
50g good milk chocolate
100g 72% dark chocolate
gold leaf, to decorate
  (optional)

For the caramel
225g golden caster sugar
125ml double cream
25g butter
pinch of salt flakes
100g toasted flaked
  almonds

A buttery biscuit topped with caramel and chocolate. Could there be anything better?

Heat the oven to 160°C/Fan 140°C/Gas 3 and butter and line a 20 x 20cm tin. Mix the flour, almonds, rice flour, sugar and a pinch of salt together in a food processor. Whizz in 150g of the butter in batches to make a dough, then tip it into the tin and press down with your hands. Chill for 10 minutes then bake for 30–35 minutes until lightly golden. Leave to cool in the tin.

To make the caramel, tip the sugar into a frying pan and heat it gently so it starts to melt. Tip the pan to make sure one side doesn't start to brown before the other. Keep heating and tipping until you have golden caramel. Add the cream carefully, stirring all the time, then reheat and stir to make a smooth sauce. Add the butter, a pinch of salt flakes and the flaked almonds and then pour the sauce (warm it again if you need to) over the shortbread. Leave to cool.

Meanwhile, heat the chocolates together with the remaining butter in a pan and pour this over the cooled caramel. When the chocolate is firm but still sticky, add some pieces of gold leaf randomly across the surface, if you like. Leave to cool but cut into pieces while the chocolate is still a little soft.

Per square 364 kcals, **protein** 4g, **carbohydrate** 28.5g, **fat** 25.7g, **saturated fat** 12.4g, **fibre** 0.8g, **salt** 0.3g

Nut and oat breakfast bars

1 hour, plus cooling | makes 16 | easy

250g jumbo oats

50g hazelnuts, roughly
chopped

20g coconut flakes
(unsweetened, not
desiccated)

130g crunchy peanut
butter

130ml brown rice syrup

1 egg

1 tsp ground ginger

6 Brazil nuts, roughly
chopped

20g puffed rice

20g raisins

20g dried soured cherries

This recipe makes a good base for using whichever nuts and dried fruit you like. You can also add chia, flax or other seeds, but don't increase the volume of dry ingredients too much or the bars won't hold together.

Heat the oven to 180°C/Fan 160°C/Gas 4. Spread the oats out on a baking sheet and toast them for 7–10 minutes, keeping an eye on them so they don't burn. Tip them into a bowl, and toast the hazelnuts and then the coconut in the same way. (The coconut will brown fast, so keep an eye on it.) Add them to the bowl. Turn the oven down to 160°C/Fan 140°C/Gas 3.

Mix the peanut butter with the rice syrup, egg and ginger. Stir this into the oats along with the Brazil nuts, puffed rice and dried fruit, and keep stirring until everything is thoroughly coated and sticky. Line a 26 x 20cm baking tin with non-stick baking paper and gently press the mixture into it, making sure it is even and level.

Bake for 25–30 minutes. The surface should be browned all over, but take care that the fruit doesn't burn. (It will puff up as it cooks, but shrink back again as it cools.) Take the tin out of the oven and cool for 15 minutes, then mark out the bars evenly on the surface of the mixture. When completely cold, lift it out of the tin and cut it into individual bars along the marked lines using a heavy, sharp knife.

Per bar 187 kcals, **protein** 6.3g, **carbohydrate** 17.9g, **fat** 9.4g, **saturated fat** 2.1g, **fibre** 3g, **salt** 0.1g

Tarts and pastries

Pear and hazelnut Bakewell

1 hour, plus cooling | serves 8 | easy

1 x 375g block sweet
  pastry
3 tbsp plain flour, plus
  extra for dusting
100g softened butter
100g golden caster sugar
2 eggs
110g hazelnuts, finely
  ground
½ tsp baking powder
zest of 1 orange
3–4 very ripe small pears
2–3 tbsp raspberry jam
2 tbsp apricot jam

Use a spice grinder to process the hazelnuts as finely as you can; adding a little sugar will help the mix stay dry.

Heat the oven to 190°C/Fan 170°C/Gas 5. Roll out the pastry on a floured work surface and use it to line a long rectangular, loose-bottomed tart tin approximately 34 x 11cm or a 22–23cm circular tin. Line with non-stick baking paper and baking beans, and bake for 15 minutes.

Meanwhile, beat the butter and sugar until creamy, then beat in the eggs, hazelnuts, flour, baking powder and orange zest.

Peel the pears, cut them in half and scoop out the cores. Put them cut-side down on a board and slice vertically through each half at 5mm intervals, leaving the pieces attached at the stem end.

When the pastry is cooked, lift out the paper and beans, then put the pastry back in the oven to dry out for a further 5 minutes. Spread the raspberry jam over the pastry base, then scoop the hazelnut mix into the pastry case. Press down carefully on the pears to fan them out a little, then lift them onto the hazelnut mixture.

Bake for 25–30 minutes or until the filling is puffed and golden. Brush the top with apricot jam and leave to cool until just warm.

Per serving 536 kcals, **protein** 7.8g, **carbohydrate** 48.4g, **fat** 33.7g, **saturated fat** 11.6, **fibre** 3.8g, **salt** 0.8g

Double chocolate brownie tart with boozy cream

1 hour 20 minutes, plus cooling | serves 8–10 | a little effort

125g salted butter, cut into
   cubes
100g 70% dark chocolate,
   chopped
150g golden caster sugar
2 eggs, beaten
4 tbsp plain flour
100g milk chocolate,
   75g cut into chunks,
   25g melted

For the chocolate pastry
200g plain flour
2 tbsp golden caster sugar
2 tbsp cocoa powder
100g salted butter, chilled
   and cubed
2 egg yolks

For the boozy cream
300ml double cream
2–3 tbsp Baileys, Tia Maria
   or Cointreau
icing sugar, to sweeten

Flavour the cream for this with whatever liqueur you fancy and serve the tart warm for maximum squidginess.

To make the pastry, whizz the flour, sugar and cocoa in a food processor. Add the butter and mix to a breadcrumb texture. Add the egg yolks and pulse to a dough (you can add a teaspoon or so of cold water if it begins to get very dry). Wrap in cling film and chill for 30 minutes.

Heat the oven to 200°C/Fan 180°C/Gas 6. Roll out the pastry between 2 pieces of baking paper (this makes it easier to handle) and use it to line a 23cm tart tin. Line the pastry case with baking paper and baking beans and bake for 10 minutes. Take out the paper and beans and cook for another 5–7 minutes. Remove the tin and lower the oven to 180°C/Fan 160°C/Gas 4.

Put the butter and dark chocolate in a heatproof bowl and melt on low power in the microwave. Cool a little then whisk in the sugar and eggs. Stir in the flour and milk chocolate chunks to combine.

Pour this mixture into the pastry case then bake for 30 minutes. Leave to cool a little then drizzle with the melted milk chocolate.

Mix the cream with the liqueur and enough icing sugar to sweeten (this will depend on which liqueur you use and how sweet you like your puddings) then whip softly. Serve alongside the warm cake.

Per serving 635 kcals, **protein** 7g, **carbohydrate** 51g, **fat** 43.8g, **saturated fat** 26.4g, **fibre** 1.6g, **salt** 0.5g

Jelly and custard cream slice

2 hours, plus setting and cooling | serves 6 | tricky but worth it

375g pack of all-butter
   puff pastry
2 tbsp icing sugar

For the berry jelly
6 gelatine leaves
500g frozen mixed berries
100g golden caster sugar
200ml water
oil, for greasing

For the icing
250g icing sugar, sifted
2½ tbsp water
a few drops of red or pink
   food colouring

For the custard cream
200ml whipping cream
150g pot of custard
125g mascarpone
2 tbsp icing sugar
1 tsp vanilla paste or
   extract

This recipe takes a classic millefeuille and gives it a very British jelly and custard treatment. Make all the elements ahead then simply assemble to serve.

To make the jelly layer, put the gelatine leaves one by one into some cold water to soften. Put the berries and sugar in a pan with the water and warm gently until the sugar has dissolved, then bring to the boil for 2 minutes. Take the berries off the heat and mash well, then press them through a sieve into a measuring jug – you need 500ml of liquid. Squeeze the excess water out of the softened gelatine, then stir it into the berry juice until dissolved. Brush the inside of a 22cm square tin with a little oil, line with a double layer of cling film then pour in the berry jelly and chill until set.

Heat the oven to 200°C/Fan 180°C/Gas 6. Roll out the pastry on a sheet of baking parchment to a 30 x 35cm rectangle. Dust with the icing sugar and lay over a second sheet of baking parchment. Lift onto a flat baking sheet and sit another flat baking sheet on top, like a sandwich. Fill a few small tins with baking beans (or something similarly heavy and ovenproof, such as raw rice) and put these on top. Bake for 30 minutes, then have a quick peek – it will probably need another 5 minutes to be well-browned and crisp all over, but it's best to check. Lift the pastry from the oven and carefully remove the weights, top tin and top sheet of parchment. Leave to cool.

When the pastry is cool, use a big, sharp knife and ruler to cut the pastry into two 10 x 24cm neat rectangles, and a third rectangle about 12 x 26cm. Divide each of the 10 x 24cm rectangles into six so you end up with twelve 10 x 4cm pieces. Mix the icing sugar for the icing with the water to make a thick, runny icing. Remove a couple of spoonfuls and mix with enough colouring to get a deep pink colour, then transfer this to a small piping bag.

Spread the white icing over the 12 x 26cm pastry rectangle, then pipe across thin stripes of the pink icing. Use a skewer or toothpick to drag lines through the icing, at right angles to the pink stripes, to feather it. Leave the pastry in the fridge until the icing is set hard. Cover the other pastry with cling film to keep it crisp and fresh.

Whip the cream, custard, mascarpone, icing sugar and vanilla together until the mixture is just holding its shape, then spoon it into a big piping bag. Chill until you're ready to assemble.

To assemble, carefully lift the jelly from its tin. Halve, then divide each half into 6 rectangles; the easiest way to do this is with a big pair of kitchen scissors, cutting through both the jelly and the cling film – then you can top each portion of jelly with a piece of pastry, neatly flip so the pastry is at the bottom, and peel off the cling film. Trim the edges of the iced pastry to 10 x 24cm, then divide into six. Pipe blobs of the custard cream over each jelly-topped pastry slice, then carefully stack into six sandwiches, finishing with your iced pastry top.

Per serving 746 kcals, **protein** 7.2g, **carbohydrate** 100.1g, **fat** 35.7g, **saturated fat** 19.6g, **fibre** 2.7g, **salt** 0.6g

Raspberry lime curd tart

1 hour | serves 8 | easy

350g shortcrust pastry,
    fresh or frozen
2 tbsp plain flour, plus
    extra for dusting
3 egg yolks
125g caster sugar
50g unsalted butter, melted
250ml half-fat crème
    fraîche
zest and juice of 1 lime
pinch of salt
150g raspberries

Incredibly simple to make, the filling for this tart miraculously turns into lime curd in the oven. You could replace the raspberries with blueberries or blackberries, if you like.

Heat the oven to 200°C/Fan 180°C/Gas 6. Roll out the pastry on a floured surface to ½cm thick and use it to line a 23cm loose-based tart tin. Line with non-stick baking paper and baking beans or dried beans and blind bake for 10 minutes. Remove the baking paper and bake for 5 more minutes or until the pastry looks dry and lightly golden. Turn the oven down to 180°C/Fan 160°C/Gas 4.

Whisk the egg yolks, sugar, melted butter, crème fraîche, flour, lime zest and juice together in a bowl with a pinch of salt and pour the mixture into the pastry case.

Sprinkle the raspberries over the top and cook for 30–40 minutes, or until the filling is just set. Allow to cool in the tin completely on a cooling rack and serve at room temperature or chilled with cream or ice cream.

Per serving 402 kcal, **protein** 5.3g, **carbohydrate** 42.1g, **fat** 24.7g, **saturated fat** 11.7g, **fibre** 1.4g, **salt** 0.49g

Espresso tart with hazelnut pastry and Kahlúa cream

1¼ hours, plus chilling | serves 8 | a little effort

140g plain flour
50g ground hazelnuts
30g golden caster sugar
100g butter, chilled and
   diced
1 egg, separated

For the filling
300ml double cream
1 tbsp light muscovado
   sugar
1 tbsp espresso powder
200g dark chocolate,
   chopped
50g butter
2 tbsp Kahlúa

For the Kahlúa cream
125ml double cream
1 tbsp icing sugar
1 tbsp Kahlúa

You only need a slice of this rich tart to sate your cravings. It makes a simple yet elegant dinner party dessert too.

Put the flour, hazelnuts and sugar in a food processor or bowl and whizz or rub in the butter until the mixture looks like breadcrumbs.

Add the egg yolk and pulse or mix until you have a rough dough (add a little very cold water to combine if needed). Bring the dough together with your hands and knead it briefly on a floured surface, then roll it out and use it to line a rectangular 35 x 12cm tart tin or a 24cm round tart tin (you may need to patch it up a bit with some pastry scraps). Leave some pastry sticking up above the sides of the tin and chill the pastry case for 30 minutes.

Heat the oven to 190°C/Fan 170°C/Gas 5. Line the pastry with baking paper or foil and baking beans, and bake for 15–20 minutes. Take out the baking paper or foil, brush the pastry with the egg white and bake for another 5 minutes. Trim off the excess pastry and cool the case completely.

Heat the cream, sugar and espresso powder to just below boiling point and pour the mixture over the chopped chocolate and butter, stirring until the chocolate is melted. Whisk in the Kahlúa. Pour the mix into the tart and leave to set at a cool room temperature or in the fridge.

To serve, whisk the cream with the icing sugar and Kahlúa to just beyond soft peaks. Spoon it into a pastry bag fitted with a round, straight-edged nozzle and pipe small dots on top of the tart.

Per serving 706 kcals, **protein** 6.6g, **carbohydrate** 31.4g, **fat** 59.5g, **saturated fat** 34.1g, **fibre** 4g, **salt** 0.4g

Pecan, maple and bourbon tart with pecan pastry

1 hour, plus chilling | serves 10 | a little effort

100g unsalted butter

½ tsp salt

100g light brown muscovado sugar

3 eggs

150ml maple syrup, plus extra to serve (optional)

1 tsp vanilla extract

2 tbsp bourbon

270g pecan halves

For the pastry

150g plain flour, plus extra for dusting

pinch of salt

2 tbsp golden caster sugar

75g unsalted butter, chilled and cubed

2 egg yolks (save 1 egg white, for sealing the pastry)

30g pecan halves

A dash of bourbon ramps up the flavour of this sticky tart.

To make the pastry, pulse the flour, a pinch of salt, sugar and butter in a food processor to fine breadcrumbs. Add the egg yolks and blitz again briefly. Now add the pecans and pulse, just until the pastry starts to come together. Turn out onto a cool surface and knead very briefly. Chill for 20 minutes.

Roll the pastry out between two pieces of non-stick baking paper to stop it sticking (or lightly flour the surface and rolling pin instead) to form a large rectangle. Use the pastry to line a 20 x 30cm rectangular tart tin with a removable base or a round 23cm tart tin. Press the pastry into the corners and edges – the pastry is very short so you may need to do a bit of patching up if it breaks. Trim the pastry edges flush with the tin, prick the base all over with a fork and put it back in the fridge to chill for at least 30 minutes.

Heat the oven to 190°C/Fan 170°C/Gas 5. Line the pastry case with baking paper and fill with baking beans. Bake for 10 minutes then remove the paper and beans and cook for 5–8 minutes, until it looks biscuity but is still very pale. Brush the base with a light coating of egg white to seal.

To make the filling, whisk the butter, salt and sugar for a few minutes, until light and airy. Whisk in the eggs, one at a time, followed by the maple syrup, vanilla and bourbon. Pour into the pastry case and arrange the pecans on top, in a snug layer.

Bake for 10 minutes, then reduce the oven temperature to 180°C/ Fan 160°C/Gas 4 and cook for a further 35 minutes or until risen and just set. Serve warm or cool with cream and extra maple syrup, if you like.

Per serving 522 kcals, **protein** 6.8g, **carbohydrate** 35.8g, **fat** 38.2g, **saturated fat** 11.5g, **fibre** 2.5g, **salt** 0.2g

Apple and Cheddar crust pie

1½ hours | serves 8 | easy

2 small Bramley apples, peeled, cored and sliced
3–4 dessert apples, peeled, cored and sliced
zest of 1 lemon
2 tsp cornflour
good grating of nutmeg
3 tbsp golden caster sugar
1 egg, beaten

For the pastry
150g butter, chopped and very cold
50g lard, chopped and very cold
450g plain flour
150g Cheddar, finely grated
3–4 tbsp cold water

Sweet and savoury, this pie satisfies a multitude of cravings.

First make the pastry by rubbing the butter and lard into the flour until you have a mixture that looks like crumbs. Add the Cheddar and cold water, and mix everything to a dough. Knead briefly, then press it out into a disc, wrap it in cling film and chill for 30 minutes.

Heat the oven to 200°C/Fan 180°C/Gas 6. Roll out just over half of the pastry thinly and use it to line a rectangular metal pie plate about 20 x 15cm or a round 23cm diameter tin, leaving any extra pastry hanging over the edge.

Tip all the apples into a bowl and add the lemon zest, cornflour, a good grating of nutmeg and the sugar. Turn everything over with your hands until the cornflour is well distributed, then arrange the filling neatly in the pie dish, building it up in the centre.

Roll out the remaining half of the pastry to make a lid. Cut the pastry into strips and weave them together to make a lattice. Brush around the edge of the pie plate with water and lift the lattice onto it. Press the edges together and trim away any excess pastry, keeping the edge as neat as you can. Cut a steam hole in the centre if there are no holes in the lattice. Brush the pastry with the egg and bake the pie for 45–50 minutes or until the pastry is golden and browned, and the filling is bubbling through the steam hole.

Per serving 548 kcals, **protein** 11.6g, **carbohydrate** 56.7g, **fat** 29.7g, **saturated fat** 16.7g, **fibre** 3.8g, **salt** 0.7g

Pumpkin pie with maple cream

1½ hours | serves 8 | easy

500g shortcrust pastry
a large pinch of cinnamon
800g pumpkin, peeled and
  chopped
150ml single cream
150g light muscovado
  sugar
a good grating of nutmeg
a pinch of ground ginger
3 eggs
30g butter, melted

For the maple cream
150ml double cream
3 tbsp maple syrup

The best pumpkin pie. Designed to impress, this rich, creamy pud uses bought pastry, making it easy but still a special bake. Maple cream goes on the side. Choose firmer fleshed, sweet pumpkin such as butternut squash, acorn or kabocha for this – the latter is the least sweet.

Roll out the pastry and line a 20cm round tart tin, trimming the edges (keep the excess pastry for decoration). Sprinkle the cinnamon onto the pastry. Chill for 30 minutes.

Meanwhile, put the pumpkin, single cream, sugar, nutmeg and ginger in a saucepan and bring to a simmer. Cook gently with the lid half on for about 20 minutes, or until the pumpkin is tender, then purée the lot and cool the mixture until warm.

Heat the oven to 200°C/Fan 180°C/Gas 6. Line the tart case with baking paper or foil and fill with baking beans, then bake the pastry blind for 15 minutes. Remove the paper and beans and bake for a further 5 minutes or until the base is dry and cooked. Turn the oven down to 180°C/Fan 160°C/Gas 4.

Beat the eggs and butter into the purée and pour the mixture into the pastry case (you might have a bit of mix left over depending on the depth of your case). Cut pastry shapes out of the extra pastry, if you like, and use them to decorate the edges of the tart – don't put them in the centre or they will sink. Bake for 30 minutes and then check the tart – it should have a slight wobble in the centre. Cook for another 10 minutes if it's too runny.

Beat the double cream until thick then beat in the maple syrup to combine. Serve with the pie.

Per serving 585 kcals, **protein** 7.9g, **carbohydrate** 54.4g, **fat** 36.6g, **saturated fat** 16.7g, **fibre** 2.9g, **salt** 0.8g

Lemon meringue pies

1 hour, plus cooling | serves 6 | a little effort

350g sweet dessert pastry
(look for an all-butter
variety)

For the meringue
2 egg whites
100g caster sugar

For the lemon filling
2 level tbsp cornflour
100g caster sugar
zest of 2 large lemons
175ml lemon juice
150ml water
85g butter, chilled and
diced
3 egg yolks plus 1 whole
egg, beaten

This is a great way to make use of lemons. The meringue in the recipe turns golden in the oven so there's no need to use a blowtorch.

Heat the oven to 190°C/Fan 170°C/Gas 5. Roll out the pastry to the thickness of a 20p piece. Put six tart rings (about 10cm in diameter) on a large baking sheet and line with the pastry, leaving the sides overhanging a little to prevent shrinkage (or use 10cm tart tins). Fill each ring with scrunched-up baking paper and beans and bake blind for 10 minutes. Take out the beans and paper and cook for another 5–10 minutes until there are no uncooked pastry patches. Trim the edges flush with the tart rings.

To make the lemon filling, mix the cornflour, sugar and lemon zest in a pan. Sift in the lemon juice gradually, then stir in the water. Cook over a medium heat, stirring constantly, until thickened and smooth. Once the mixture bubbles, remove from the heat and beat in the butter until melted.

Stir the egg yolks and egg into the pan and return to a low heat. Keep stirring for a few minutes, until the mixture thickens and just bubbles. Take off the heat and leave to cool a little then divide the filling between the pastry cases.

Put the egg whites in a clean bowl, whisk to soft peaks then start adding the sugar a tablespoon at a time, whisking each one in. Keep going until all the sugar is used up and the meringue is stiff and shiny.

Pile spoonfuls of the meringue on top of the filling. Put the tarts back in the oven for 10–15 minutes until the meringue is peaked with gold. Cool completely before serving.

Per pie 586 kcals, **protein** 7.2g, **carbohydrate** 66.6g, **fat** 34.2g, **saturated fat** 14.7g, **fibre** 1.1g, **salt** 0.67g

Rose and almond choux buns

1½ hours, plus cooling and freezing | makes 10 | a little effort

175ml water

75g unsalted butter, chilled and diced

1 tsp golden caster sugar

½ tsp salt

100g plain flour

3 medium eggs

For the almond crumble

75g ground almonds

75g caster sugar

50g unsalted butter, chilled and diced

For the filling and decoration

250g strawberries

½–1 tbsp rose water

300ml double cream

5 tbsp icing sugar, for dusting

a few sugared rose petals for decorating (optional)

Bite-sized rose water cream buns, designed to impress. These crumble-topped treats are a doddle once you've mastered the choux.

For the almond crumble, rub the almonds, sugar and butter together to breadcrumbs, then press together to make a dough. Roll out between two sheets of baking paper as thinly as you can, then put in the freezer for 1 hour.

To make the choux buns, heat the oven to 180°C/Fan 160°C/Gas 4. Line a large baking sheet with non-stick baking paper and draw on 10 well-spaced circles that are 4cm wide (use a cookie cutter, lid or template as a guide). Flip the paper over. Put the water, butter, sugar and salt in a medium saucepan. Gently heat until the butter has melted, then turn up the heat and bring to a fierce rolling boil. Lift off the heat, tip in the flour and beat with a wooden spoon to a smooth paste. Return to a low heat and continue beating for 1–2 minutes more to dry out the mixture. Cool for 5 minutes.

Beat in two of the eggs, one by one, and continue until you have a smooth dough each time. Beat the third egg with a fork in a separate bowl, then beat in a dribble of this at a time until you have a very thick dough – you may not need all the egg. Transfer to a piping bag, fitted with a large round nozzle, or snip the end off a disposable bag. Pipe rounds of the dough onto the prepared tray, using the circles as templates. Remove the almond crumble from the freezer and using a 5cm cookie cutter, stamp out 10 discs from the frozen crumble. Sit a disc on each round of dough and bake for 40 minutes. Turn off the oven but leave the buns inside until fully cooled.

Whizz 200g of the strawberries and the rose water in a food processor until smooth. Beat the cream and icing sugar until thick, then gently fold in the strawberry purée. Slice the remaining strawberries very thinly. Halve the buns and arrange a few strawberry slices on each. Spoon or pipe the cream on them, then sandwich with the tops. Dust with a little icing sugar to serve and a few sugared rose petals if you like.

Per bun 406 kcals, **protein** 5g, **carbohydrate** 25.2g, **fat** 32.1g, **saturated fat** 17.2g, **fibre** 0.8g, **salt** 0.1g

Gooseberry sugar-crust pie

2 hours, plus chilling | serves 8 | easy

1kg gooseberries, topped and tailed

150–200g light muscovado sugar (depending on sweetness of the gooseberries)

2 tbsp elderflower cordial

1 tbsp ground almonds

1 tbsp breadcrumbs

1 egg, lightly beaten

3 tbsp demerara sugar

For the pastry

200g cold butter, cubed

250g plain flour, plus extra for dusting

2 tbsp light muscovado sugar

120g crème fraîche

This gooseberry sugar-crust pie is a great alternative to apple or rhubarb for the summer months and it looks stunning. Use a mix of pink- and green-skinned gooseberries in the filling for a variety of colour.

To make the pastry, whizz the butter, flour and sugar together in a food processor until it looks like fine breadcrumbs. Add the crème fraîche and whizz until the mix starts to clump together. Bring the pastry together on a floured surface and divide it into two portions: the first approximately one-third of the mixture, the other two-thirds. Flatten each into a disc, wrap in cling film and chill for 20 minutes.

Meanwhile, put the fruit, sugar and cordial in a wide pan and bring it to a simmer. Cook for 10 minutes, or until the gooseberries are soft.

Heat the oven to 220°C/Fan 200°C/Gas 7. Roll out the large piece of pastry on a floured surface and use it to line a pie dish 25cm wide and about 5cm deep, leaving a lip around the rim. Scatter the almonds and breadcrumbs over the base of the pie. Lift the gooseberries out of the pan with a slotted spoon and put them in the pie dish. Reduce the juice in the pan until you have about 4 tablespoons left. Spoon the juices over the gooseberries.

Roll out the remaining pastry into a circle big enough to fit the top of the pie with some overhang. Brush the lip of the bottom piece of pastry with beaten egg and lift the lid on top, pressing down around the edges. Trim the edges and then crimp them together.

Make a small hole in the top of the pie, brush the pastry all over with the egg and then scatter over the demerara. Bake for 10 minutes, then turn the oven down to 190°C/Fan 170°C/Gas 5 and bake for a further 30–40 minutes, or until the pastry looks dark golden brown. Leave the pie to rest for 20 minutes before trying to cut it. Serve with cream or custard.

Per serving 563 kcals, **protein** 5.5g, **carbohydrate** 69.7g, **fat** 28g, **saturated fat** 17.4g, **fibre** 5.3g, **salt** 0.5g

Little Linzer tarts

45 minutes, plus chilling and cooling | makes 8 | a little effort

50g blanched hazelnuts
100g blanched almonds
225g unsalted butter, softened
150g golden caster sugar
2 medium egg yolks, beaten
1 tsp vanilla extract
grated zest of ½ unwaxed lemon
250g plain flour, plus extra for dusting
½ tsp baking powder
½ tsp ground cinnamon
pinch of salt
8 heaped tsp raspberry jam
icing sugar, to serve

This is a version of a classic Austrian tart from the town of Linz. With buttery, nutty pastry, these are jam tarts for grown ups. Use blueberry, blackcurrant, cherry or plum jam – whatever takes your fancy.

Tip the hazelnuts and almonds into a food processor and pulse until finely ground. Beat the butter with the caster sugar until pale, light and fluffy. Add the egg yolks, vanilla and lemon zest and mix. Sift together the plain flour, baking powder, cinnamon and a pinch of salt. Add the flour mixture to the creamed mixture with the ground almonds and hazelnuts and mix until combined. Lightly knead the mixture until it comes together into a ball, then flatten it into a disc, wrap in cling film and chill for 1 hour or until firm.

On a lightly floured work surface roll two-thirds of the dough out to a thickness of 2–3mm. Stamp out 8 discs using an 11cm fluted cutter. Carefully push the dough into 8 individual 10cm tart tins, making sure that the dough is evenly placed in the tins and comes about 2–3mm up the sides. Spoon 1 heaped teaspoon of jam into the middle of each pastry case and spread to the edges. Roll out the remaining dough and cut it into thin strips. Brush the edge of each pastry case with a drop of cold water and arrange the pastry strips in a lattice across each tart. Chill for 30 minutes.

Heat the oven to 160°C/Fan 140°C/Gas 3. Put the tins on a solid baking sheet and bake the tarts on the middle shelf of the oven for about 10–12 minutes or until golden brown. Leave to cool in the tins for 5 minutes and then carefully lift out onto a wire cooling rack. Dust with icing sugar to serve.

Per serving 563 kcals, **protein** 7.6g, **carbohydrate** 542g, **fat** 36g, **saturated fat** 16g, **fibre** 2.3g, **salt** 0.4g

Panna cotta tart with roasted plums

1 hour 20 minutes, plus cooling and chilling | serves 8 | a little effort

250g plain flour, plus extra
   for dusting
75g icing sugar
pinch of salt
150g unsalted butter,
   chilled and diced
2 medium eggs (1 whole
   and 1 separated)
800g ripe plums
1 vanilla pod
1 cinnamon stick
juice of 1 large orange
2 tbsp clear honey

For the panna cotta
4 gelatine leaves
1 vanilla pod or 1 tsp
   vanilla bean paste
450ml double cream
1 strip of lemon peel
450g fromage frais
75g golden caster sugar

The filling for this panna cotta can also be used in ramekins, if you like. If you can't find plain fromage frais you could try substituting it with crème fraîche or goat's milk yoghurt.

To make the pastry, tip the flour, icing sugar and a pinch of salt into the bowl of a food processor. Add the butter and pulse until the mixture looks like coarse sand. Add 1 whole egg and 1 egg yolk (you'll need the white later) and mix briefly to bring the dough together. Tip the dough out and very lightly knead it into a smooth ball. Flatten into a disc, wrap in cling film and chill for 1 hour.

Roll out the dough on a surface lightly dusted with flour and use to line a 23cm loose-bottomed tart tin. Allow the excess pastry to hang over the edges. Prick the base of the tart with a fork and chill on a baking sheet for at least 30 minutes.

Heat the oven to 180°C/Fan 160°C/Gas 4. Line the tart shell with baking paper, fill with baking beans and bake blind until golden and crisp – this should take about 20 minutes. Remove the baking paper and baking beans, brush the inside of the tart shell with the reserved egg white and trim off the excess pastry. Return the tart to the oven for a further 3–4 minutes to crisp and dry out the base. Leave to cool completely. Leave the oven on.

To cook the plums, cut them into halves and quarters and remove the stones. Arrange them in a baking dish cut-side up, tuck the vanilla pod and cinnamon stick among the fruit, pour over the orange juice and drizzle with the honey. Bake in the oven for about 20 minutes (depending on ripeness) until tender but not falling apart. Leave the fruit to cool completely.

To make the filling, soak the gelatine leaves in a bowl of cold water for 10 minutes. Halve the vanilla pod and scrape out the seeds, then put the pod and seeds into a saucepan with the cream and lemon peel and slowly bring to the boil. Take off the heat and leave to infuse for 10 minutes.

Bring the cream back to the boil, strain into a bowl and discard the vanilla pod and lemon peel. Drain the gelatine leaves, squeeze out excess water and drop them into the hot cream. Whisk to dissolve then add the fromage frais and sugar and whisk until combined. Pour into the tart shell and slide carefully into the fridge for 2 hours or until the panna cotta has set. Serve the tart with the plums spooned over the top.

Per serving 732 kcals, **protein** 10.2g, **carbohydrate** 56.5g, **fat** 51.7g, **saturated fat** 31.9g, **fibre** 3.4g, **salt** 0.2g

Peach Melba tart

1½ hours, plus chilling | serves 8 | a little effort

4 ripe but firm peaches

284ml pot single cream

½ vanilla pod, split
   lengthways

2 eggs (1 whole and 1 yolk)

40g golden caster sugar,
   plus 3 tbsp

2 good handfuls of
   raspberries

2 tbsp flaked almonds,
   toasted

For the pastry

250g plain flour, plus extra
   for dusting

1 tbsp golden caster sugar

150g butter, chilled and
   diced

1 egg, beaten

With peaches and raspberries baked in a smooth, creamy custard, this modern version of the classic peach Melba is sure to be a hit.

Heat the oven to 200°C/Fan 180°C/Gas 6. To make the pastry, put the flour, sugar and butter in a food processor and blend until the mixture resembles fine breadcrumbs. With the motor running, slowly add the egg and blend just long enough for the mixture to form a ball.

Transfer the dough to a lightly floured surface and roll out into a circle roughly 25cm in diameter. Use the pastry to line a 23cm-deep, loose-based, fluted quiche tin. Put the tin on a sturdy baking sheet and chill for 30 minutes.

Line the tart case with a large piece of crumpled baking paper and fill with baking beans. Bake in the centre of the oven for 25 minutes. Remove from the oven and discard the paper and beans. Return the pastry case to the oven for a further 3 minutes until the base is dry. Reduce the oven temperature to 150°C/Fan 130°C/Gas 2. While the pastry is baking blind, prepare the filling. Slice the peaches and twist in half. Remove the stones. Put the peach halves in a pan, cover with water and bring to the boil, then blanch the fruit for 1 minute. Remove with a slotted spoon and when cool enough to handle, peel off the skin. Drain the peaches on kitchen paper.

Pour the cream into a saucepan, scrape in the vanilla seeds and throw in the empty pod for good measure. Place the pan over a medium heat and bring to a simmer for 10 seconds. Beat the egg and egg yolk with the sugar in a bowl until creamed. Remove the vanilla pod from the cream and pour the cream over the eggs, whisking vigorously until thoroughly mixed.

Arrange the peach halves, cut-side down, in the part-cooked pastry case. Dot with the raspberries then pour over the custard – it should almost reach the top of the pastry. Return to the oven and bake for about 45 minutes or until the custard is just set – it should still wobble in the middle. Cool in the tin. Scatter over with some toasted flaked almonds and serve.

Per serving 500 kcals, **protein** 7.4g, **carbohydrate** 43.6g, **fat** 34.1g, **saturated fat** 19.4g, **fibre** 2.4g, **salt** 0.38g

Cherry blondie tart

1½ hours | serves 12 | easy

300g shortcrust pastry
50g dark chocolate
200g cherries, pitted
  and halved, plus a few
  whole cherries reserved
  for the top
100g golden caster sugar
2 eggs
100g butter, melted
100g plain flour
100g white chocolate,
  finely chopped
3 tbsp icing sugar

A delicious recipe for a chocolate tart. Ready-made pastry makes this easy, but it's still special enough to serve to friends and family. Cherries and white chocolate are a surprisingly good combination.

Heat the oven to 200°C/Fan 180°C/Gas 6. Roll out the pastry and line a 22–23cm tart tin. Bake blind for 20 minutes, then remove the baking paper and beans and dry the base out by baking it for 5 minutes more. Lower the oven heat to 180°C/Fan 160°C/Gas 4.

Melt the dark chocolate in the microwave or in a heatproof bowl set over a pan of simmering water, making sure the base of the bowl does not touch the water. Brush the melted chocolate all over the pastry base and top with most of the cherries.

Beat the caster sugar and eggs together until the mixture is fluffy, then beat in the butter in three additions. Fold in the flour and white chocolate pieces and pour the mixture into the tart case. Bake for 40 minutes or until the top stops wobbling when you give the tin a gentle shake. Allow to cool a little until warm, rather than hot.

Remove the tart from the tin and put it on a serving plate. Mix the icing sugar with enough water to make a spoonable icing and pipe or spoon it across the tart, running it back and forth. Decorate the top with the extra cherries.

Per serving 340 kcals, **protein** 4.4g, **carbohydrate** 37.3g, **fat** 19.3g, **saturated fat** 19.3g, **fibre** 1.6g, **salt** 0.4g

Passion fruit tart with meringue

1 hour 45 minutes | serves 8 | easy

375g sweet pastry
8 large or 10 small passion
   fruit
300g golden caster sugar
6 eggs, separated
150ml double cream

This zingy tart is an easy way to cook with passion fruit. The meringue topping adds a twist to the traditional recipe.

Heat the oven to 180°C/Fan 160°C/Gas 4. Roll out the pastry and use it to line a 23cm tart ring. Chill for 20 minutes then line it with baking paper and baking beans or uncooked rice and bake for 10 minutes. Lift out the paper and beans and return the pastry to the oven for 10 minutes to dry out the base. Turn the oven down to 140°C/Fan 120°C/Gas 1.

Cut the passion fruit in half and scoop out the pulp and seeds into a sieve set over a jug, then stir with a wooden spoon until all the pulp has been pushed through. Mix 150g of the sugar with the egg yolks then stir in the cream followed by the passion fruit and pour everything into the pastry case. Bake for 30 minutes or until just set but still wobbly. Take the tart out of the oven and turn the heat back up to 180°C/Fan 160°C/Gas 4.

Ten minutes before the tart is ready, beat three of the egg whites to stiff peaks and beat in the remaining sugar to make a shiny meringue. Pipe rosettes or blobs of meringue all over the top of the pie and bake for 5–10 minutes (or use a blowtorch) until the tips of the meringue peaks are lightly browned.

Per serving 516 kcals, **protein** 8.1g, **carbohydrate** 59.7g, **fat** 27.5g, **saturated fat** 11.6g, **fibre** 2g, **salt** 0.6g

Lemon curd and blackberry tart

1 hour, plus setting | serves 8 | a little effort

350g sweet pastry
6 eggs
225g caster sugar
juice and zest of
    4 unwaxed lemons
250ml double cream

For the blackberry layer
2 leaves of gelatine
200g blackberries
2 tbsp caster sugar
75ml water

This looks patisserie-perfect but is quite achievable with a little patience. Make sure you cool the lemon layer completely before you add the jelly.

Roll the pastry out and use it to line a 20 x 3cm deep straight-sided tart tin, tart ring or shallow loose-based sponge tin, leaving the pastry overhanging. Prick the base with a fork and chill for 20 minutes.

Heat the oven to 180°C/Fan 160°C/Gas 4 and put in a baking sheet. Line the tart with baking paper and baking beans and blind bake on the baking sheet for 15–20 minutes or until it is pale golden brown. Take out the paper and beans and cook for a further 4–5 minutes. Cool, then trim the excess pastry. Turn the oven down to 150°C/Fan 130°C/Gas 2.

To make the filling, whisk the eggs, sugar and lemon juice until smooth. Strain through a sieve, then mix in the lemon zest and cream. Pour the mixture into the case, making sure you leave a gap of approximately ¾cm between the filling and the top of the pastry (you might have a little left over depending on the size of your tin). Put it back in the oven for 30–35 minutes or until the filling is set. Leave to cool completely in the tin.

To make the blackberry layer, soften the gelatine in cold water for 10 minutes, then squeeze out all the excess water. Meanwhile, put the blackberries, sugar and water in a pan. Heat gently until the sugar dissolves then simmer for 5 minutes. Push the mixture through a sieve into a jug and measure out 150ml of liquid. Pour this back into the pan, reheat, then take the pan off the heat and stir in the softened gelatine until dissolved. Pour into a bowl and cool.

When the mixture is cool and starting to thicken, pour it on top of the tart and put the tart in the fridge for about 1–2 hours or until set.

Per serving 523 kcals, **protein** 8g, **carbohydrate** 56.1g, **fat** 29.2g, **saturated fat** 15.8g, **fibre** 1.9g, **salt** 0.4g

Dark chocolate and salted caramel tart

1 hour 50 minutes | serves 8 | a little effort

200g plain flour

2 tbsp sugar

2 tbsp cocoa powder

100g butter

2 egg yolks

a few drops of vanilla
extract

For the caramel

250g caster sugar

5 tbsp water

125g salted butter

100ml single cream

a pinch of sea salt flakes

For the chocolate layer

2 tbsp sugar

2 eggs, 1 whole, 1 egg yolk

100g plain chocolate

75g unsalted butter

Salted caramel adds sweetness to bitter dark chocolate and adds a touch of luxury for a dinner party dessert.

Preheat the oven to 200°C/Fan 180°C/Gas 6. Whizz the flour, sugar and cocoa powder in a food processor. Add the butter and whizz until the mixture resembles breadcrumbs. Add the egg yolks and vanilla and whizz to a dough. Put the dough on a plate and press into a disc. Wrap it in cling film and chill for 30 minutes.

Roll out the pastry and line a deep 20cm tart tin with it, patching any holes if needed. Cover and chill for at least 30 minutes.

Meanwhile, to make the caramel, dissolve the sugar in the water in a large pan. Stir in the butter, raise the heat a little, and bubble, stirring occasionally until it turns a light toffee colour – this may take about 20 minutes. Turn off the heat and stir in half the cream. When the bubbles die down, stir in the rest of the cream and a pinch of sea salt flakes. Leave to cool.

Prick the base of the tart with a fork. Take a long piece of foil and scrunch it into a sausage. Curl it into a circle and fit it inside the tart, pressing against the sides of the tart to hold them up as it cooks. Bake for 12 minutes, until the pastry looks dry and cooked.

Turn the heat down to 190°C/Fan 170°C/Gas 5. To make the chocolate layer, beat the sugar, egg and egg yolk together with an electric whisk until thick and custard-coloured. Melt the chocolate and butter together in a pan, pour this into the egg mixture and beat everything until smooth and glossy.

Spread the caramel over the base of the tart, then spoon the chocolate mixture over the top, spreading it evenly. Bake for 12 minutes, then leave to cool in the tin. Serve in slices.

Per serving 653 kcals, **protein** 5.9g, **carbohydrate** 69.6g, **fat** 40.9g, **saturated fat** 24.2g, **fibre** 1.3g, **salt** 0.53g

Mini treats

Cinnamon buns

3 hours 20 minutes | makes 7 | a little effort

175ml whole milk

2 tsp dried active yeast

35g golden caster sugar

350g strong white bread flour, plus extra for dusting

½ tsp salt

2 eggs, beaten

50g unsalted butter, very soft, plus extra for greasing

demerara sugar, for dusting

For the cinnamon butter

100g unsalted butter, very soft

2 tbsp golden caster sugar

3 tsp ground cinnamon

Sticky and sweet, cinnamon buns are a Scandinavian and North American favourite, served for breakfast or as a satisfying snack. Also known as cinnamon swirls or cinnamon rolls, these are delicious treats for friends and family.

Heat the milk to just below boiling point then take it off the heat and leave to cool until warm. Whisk in the dried yeast and 1 teaspoon of the caster sugar and leave in a warm place for about 10 minutes or until a thick foam has formed on top of the milk.

Tip the flour into a large mixing bowl and stir in the salt and the rest of the caster sugar. Make a well in the middle of the flour and pour in the yeasty milk mixture, half the beaten egg and the soft butter. Stir until the mixture is combined and comes together into a dough. Tip the dough onto a lightly-floured worksurface and knead for 5 minutes until the dough is smooth and elastic. Form into a ball, put it in a bowl and cover with cling film. Leave in a warm place for about 1½ hours. To make the cinnamon butter, beat together the butter, sugar and cinnamon.

Turn the dough out onto a lightly-floured work surface and knead gently for 30 seconds. Roll into a rectangle, measuring about 30 x 50cm. Turn it so the longest side is nearest to you, then spread the cinnamon butter over the dough, leaving a border of about 1cm around the edges.

Roll the dough up, starting with the long side closest to you and keeping the roll even. Cut the dough into 7 slices of even thickness and put them in a greased non-stick 23cm springform tin.

Cover the buns loosely with oiled cling film and leave them in a warm place for 40 minutes to prove. Heat the oven to 180°C/Fan 160°C/Gas 4. Brush the buns with the remaining beaten egg and sprinkle with demerara sugar and flour. Bake on the middle shelf of the oven for 35–40 minutes until browned and cooked through.

Per bun 410 kcals, **protein** 8.6g, **carbohydrate** 47.6g, **fat** 20g, **saturated fat** 12g, **fibre** 1.2g, **salt** 0.4g

Mini jam doughnuts

1 hour, plus rising time | makes about 20 | a little effort

175ml whole milk

75g golden caster sugar

2 tsp dried active yeast

425g strong white bread flour

½ tsp salt

2 medium eggs, lightly beaten

1 tsp finely grated orange zest

75g unsalted butter, softened

4–5 tbsp strawberry jam

For the sugar coating

25g unsalted butter, melted

6 tbsp caster sugar

If you love freshly baked doughnuts but don't want to bother with deep-frying, this is the recipe for you. Try filling your second batch with Nutella or lemon curd instead of jam.

Heat the milk to just below boiling point, then remove from the heat and cool until warm. Add 1 teaspoon of the sugar and the dried active yeast. Whisk, then leave in a warm place for 5 minutes until the yeast has formed a thick foam on top of the milk.

Tip the flour, the remaining sugar and the salt into a large mixing bowl. Make a well in the middle of the dry ingredients and add the eggs, orange zest, softened butter and yeasty milk mixture. Using a wooden spoon, mix until the mixture forms a soft dough. Tip the dough out of the bowl and knead for 5 minutes until the dough is smooth and elastic – it will be on the sticky side. Form into a ball, put it into a clean bowl, cover with cling film and leave in a warm place for about 1½ hours, or until doubled in size.

Tip the dough out onto the work surface and knead lightly again for 30 seconds and then roll out to a thickness of about 1cm. Using a 5–6cm plain round cutter, stamp out circles of dough and transfer them to baking sheets lined with non-stick baking paper, leaving plenty of space between each doughnut. Cover loosely with oiled cling film and leave in a warm place for 40 minutes, or until doubled in size.

Heat the oven to 180°C/Fan 160°C/Gas 4. Bake the doughnuts for 10–12 minutes or until golden brown. Remove from the oven and brush the doughnuts all over with melted butter, toss in the sugar and leave to cool for 15 minutes.

Spoon the jam into a disposable piping bag and snip off the end to form a small nozzle. Use a wooden skewer to make a hole in the side of each doughnut, push the piping bag into the hole and fill with about a teaspoon of jam. Serve warm or cold.

Per doughnut 174 kcals, **protein** 3.6g, **carbohydrate** 27g, **fat** 5g, **saturated fat** 3g, **fibre** 0.4g, **salt** 0.2g

Apple and raspberry breakfast muffins

35 minutes | makes 10 | easy

200g self-raising flour

50g porridge oats, plus
  1 tbsp for the top

4 tbsp soft brown sugar

½ tsp ground cinnamon

2 apples, grated

½ tsp bicarbonate of soda

2 medium eggs

150ml fat-free yoghurt

6 tbsp rapeseed oil

20 frozen raspberries

Lightly spiced and fruity, these muffins are perfect for keeping mid-morning hunger pangs at bay.

Heat the oven to 180°C/160°C Fan/Gas 4. Mix the flour, oats and 3 tablespoons of the sugar in a bowl with the cinnamon. Stir in the apples, bicarbonate of soda, eggs, yoghurt and oil and mix everything together.

Line a muffin tray with 10 paper cases and half-fill them with the mixture, then dot 2 raspberries on top of each and cover with the rest of the mixture. Mix the spare tablespoon of oats with the rest of the sugar and sprinkle over the top of the muffins. Bake for 25 minutes or until golden, risen and cooked through. Serve piping hot or cold.

Per muffin 207 kcals, **protein** 5.1g, **carbohydrate** 29.5, **fat** 8.4g, **saturated fat** 0.9g, **fibre** 1.9g, **salt** 0.40g

Pear, saffron and browned butter muffins

50 minutes | makes 12 | easy

50g butter, plus extra for
  greasing if not using cases
a pinch of saffron
185ml buttermilk or milk
140ml flavourless oil
1 egg
300g self-raising flour
¼ tsp baking powder
150g golden caster sugar
2 small pears, peeled,
  cored, cut into small
  cubes and drained on
  kitchen paper

If muffins with muffin tops are what you are after, don't use paper cases, just butter the muffin holes. These work perfectly well without the saffron if you don't have any – you could add a pinch of cinnamon or nutmeg instead, if you like.

Heat the oven to 200°C/Fan 180°C/Gas 6. Line 12 holes of a muffin tin with large paper cases or grease them. Add the saffron to the buttermilk or milk. Heat the butter in a small pan until it melts, then keep cooking until the butter starts to turn a golden brown and smells toasty. Pour it into the buttermilk and stir in the oil and egg.

Sift the flour, baking powder and sugar together. Toss the pear pieces in this mix and lift them out again. Make a well in the centre of the dry ingredients, add the buttermilk mix and fold together quickly. Fold in the pears. The mixture will be quite soft but will start to thicken as the raising agents activate.

Divide the mixture between the muffin cases or holes – they should be quite full. Bake for 20–25 minutes or until they are risen and golden on top. They may have a slightly cracked appearance, which is fine.

Per muffin 296 kcals, **protein** 3.4g, **carbohydrate** 33g, **fat** 16.6g, **saturated fat** 3.6g, **fibre** 1.8g, **salt** 0.4g

Banana and almond butter muffins

1 hour | makes 12 | easy

250g self-raising flour
1 tsp baking powder
25g ground almonds
75g light brown
   muscovado sugar
3 very ripe bananas,
   mashed
100g almond butter
2 eggs
100ml buttermilk
½ tsp vanilla extract
60g flaked almonds
125g icing sugar
juice of 1 orange

These delicious banana and almond butter muffins make a great, healthy, on-the-go breakfast. Replacing normal butter with almond butter really cuts down the calorie count as well as adding flavour.

Heat the oven to 200°C/Fan 180°C/Gas 6. Line a 12-hole muffin tin with muffin cases. Tip the flour, baking powder, almonds and sugar into a large bowl. Mix the bananas with the almond butter, eggs, buttermilk and vanilla until the mixture is smooth – use a hand blender if you have one. Fold the wet mix and dry mix together – don't worry if it looks a bit lumpy.

Divide the mixture between the cases and sprinkle a few flaked almonds onto each. Bake for 15–20 minutes, or until the muffins have risen and are golden and cracked on top. Leave to cool.

Mix the icing sugar with enough orange juice to make it sufficiently runny to spoon, but thick enough not to run off the muffins. Spoon a little onto each muffin and top with flaked almonds.

Per muffin 279 kcals, **protein** 7.2g, **carbohydrate** 39.2g, **fat** 9.9g, **saturated fat** 1g, **fibre** 2.1g, **salt** 0.3g

Pumpkin pie spiced muffins

40 minutes, plus cooling | makes 12 | easy

300g self-raising flour
2 tsp pumpkin pie spice
½ tsp baking powder
200g light muscovado
  sugar
250ml sunflower oil
4 eggs
200g pumpkin purée

For the frosting
125g butter, softened
50g icing sugar
a pinch of pumpkin pie
  spice, plus extra to dust
  (optional)
200g cream cheese

You can buy pumpkin pie spice ready mixed in the spice aisle, or mix ½ teaspoon each of cinnamon, ginger, nutmeg and allspice. For the pumpkin purée, either use tinned purée or make it by steaming and mashing butternut squash. Don't use pumpkin pie filling, though, as it has been spiced already.

Heat the oven to 180°C/Fan 160°C/Gas 4. Line 12 holes of a large muffin tin with cases. Sift the flour, pumpkin pie spice and baking powder into a large bowl and stir in the sugar.

Mix the oil, eggs and pumpkin purée together. Fold this into the dry mixture, taking care not to overmix or you'll end up with tough muffins (a few lumps are acceptable). Divide the mixture between the muffin cases and bake for 35 minutes or until cooked through. Test them with a toothpick if you're not sure – it should come out clean. Lift the muffins out of the tins and cool on a wire rack.

To make the frosting, beat the butter with the icing sugar and spice, then beat in the cream cheese. Don't overbeat or the mix will get too soft; put it in the fridge if you need to firm it up. Pipe the frosting onto the cooled muffins and sprinkle on a little extra spice, if you like.

Per muffin 541 kcals, **protein** 5.3g, **carbohydrate** 40.3g, **fat** 39.5g, **saturated fat** 13.5g, **fibre** 1.5g, **salt** 0.6g

Blueberry crumble cakes

1 hour | makes 9 | easy

30g pecans
125g very soft unsalted
    butter
125g golden caster sugar
2 eggs
125g self-raising flour
½ tsp ground cinnamon
pinch of salt
100g blueberries
1 tbsp milk

For the crumble topping
15g unsalted butter
50g self-raising flour
40g pecan nuts, roughly
    chopped
30g unrefined light brown
    sugar
¾ tsp ground cinnamon

These blueberry-packed cakes have a crunchy streusel top that complements the moist cake.

Heat the oven to 180°C/Fan 160°C/Gas 4. To make the topping, rub the butter into the flour until it resembles breadcrumbs and stir in the nuts, sugar and cinnamon. Chill while you make the cakes.

Line a 20 x 20cm square cake tin with non-stick baking paper, or if you want to use muffin tins, line each hole with a paper case.

Blitz the pecans in a mini food processor until coarsely ground. Beat the butter and sugar together until pale and fluffy, gradually beat in the eggs and sift in the flour, cinnamon and pinch of salt. Fold the spiced flour in with the ground pecans, blueberries and milk. The mixture will be quite thick but this prevents the blueberries from sinking as the cakes rise.

Pour the mixture into the cake tin or divide evenly between the paper cases. Sprinkle with the topping mixture and bake for 25–30 minutes, until risen and golden. A fine skewer inserted into the cake should come out dry with no uncooked batter stuck to it. Cool on a wire rack and once cool, cut the cake into squares.

Per cake 326 kcals, **protein** 4.3g, **carbohydrate** 34.3g, **fat** 20g, **saturated fat** 9g, **fibre** 1.2g, **salt** 0.24g

Ginger madeleines

30 minutes, plus chilling | makes 12 large or 36 small | easy

100g plain flour, plus extra
   for dusting
½ tsp baking powder
1 tsp ground ginger
pinch of salt
75g golden caster sugar
2 eggs
1 tsp vanilla extract
2 pieces of stem ginger
   from a jar, finely
   chopped, plus 1 tbsp of
   the syrup
90g unsalted butter, melted
   plus extra for greasing
1 tbsp icing sugar, for
   dusting

Dust off your madeleine tin and try this spicy twist on the classic French treat. This easy recipe has a surprisingly distinctive ginger finish – divine with a cup of hot tea.

Sift the flour, baking powder and ground ginger together with a pinch of salt. Whisk the sugar and eggs with electric beaters until they are thick and fluffy. Gently fold in the flour mix, vanilla and stem ginger and syrup. Then fold in the butter. Cover the surface of the mix with cling film and chill for 30 minutes.

Heat the oven to 200°C/Fan 180°C/Gas 6. Butter 12 ordinary madeleine tins or 36 mini ones and dust with flour. Fill each with a large blob of mixture (1 heaped tablespoon for a large mould). Bake for 10 minutes (minis will need 6) or until risen, golden and springy. Tap the tin to loosen the madeleines and tip them out. Dust with icing sugar and serve warm.

Per large madeleine 149 kcals, **protein** 2.3g, **carbohydrate** 18.7g, **fat** 7.8g, **saturated fat** 4.4g, **fibre**

Cappuccino eclairs

1 hour, plus cooling | makes 12 | a little effort

200ml water

50ml whole milk

100g unsalted butter

120g plain flour

pinch of salt

1 tbsp golden caster sugar

3 eggs, beaten

For the icing

115g fondant icing sugar

1 tbsp water

1 tsp vanilla extract

1 tsp espresso coffee
   powder for the fondant
   icing

For the cream filling

600ml double cream

1 tbsp espresso coffee
   dissolved in 2 tsp boiling
   water

1 tsp vanilla extract

1 tbsp icing sugar

The perfect pairing for breakfast or dessert. Adding milk to the choux dough gives a softer finish to the pastry.

Put the water, milk and butter in a pan, bring to a simmer and cook until the butter is completely melted. Then turn up the heat and bring to the boil. Sift the flour onto a sheet of baking paper, add a pinch of salt, then gather the two sides of the paper to make a chute and tip the contents into the pan. Quickly add the sugar and beat everything together with a wooden spoon. Turn the heat down, but keep beating until the mix turns smooth and glossy and starts to pull away from the walls of the pan. Tip the mixture into a bowl.

Once the mixture has cooled slightly, beat in the eggs a little at a time. Start with a wooden spoon then keep beating with electric beaters once the mix is less stiff. It should be smooth and stretchy and fall easily off a wooden spoon. If it reaches this stage before you've added all the eggs, don't add any more as it will be too runny to pipe.

Heat the oven to 200°C/Fan 180°C/Gas 6. Line a couple of baking sheets with non-stick baking paper, put a large nozzle (approximately 1.5cm) into a piping bag and spoon in the pastry mix. Pipe out 12 lines of the pastry about 12cm long, spaced apart. Wet your finger and press down any peaks at the end. Bake for 20–25 minutes or until golden and firm. Leave to cool, then split them in half.

To make the icing, mix the fondant icing sugar with the water, 1 teaspoon of vanilla extract and the coffee powder. The icing should be loose enough to spread over the eclairs but not so runny it drips off. Add more fondant icing sugar if you need to. Spread on the top halves of the eclairs.

Whip the cream with the dissolved coffee, vanilla extract and the icing sugar, spoon into a piping bag and pipe into the eclairs. Carefully sit the tops on and serve.

Per eclair 415 kcals, **protein** 3.9g, **carbohydrate** 20.1g, **fat** 36g, **saturated fat** 20.1g, **fibre** 0.7g, **salt** 0.09g

Butterscotch bars with toffee cream

45 minutes | makes 12 | easy

175g soft butter
175g light muscovado
   sugar
3 eggs
1 tsp vanilla extract
175g self-raising flour
100g soft toffees
75ml double cream

These neat little bars make perfect portion sizes for your family or to give out as gifts.

Heat the oven to 160°C/Fan 140°C/Gas 3. Beat the butter and sugar together until light and creamy. Beat in the eggs, vanilla and flour until you have a smooth batter. Divide the mixture between 12 bar cases (or 18 muffin cases). Bake for 15–20 minutes or until the cakes have risen and spring back when touched.

Melt 80g of the toffees with the cream, then cool until thick but spoonable. Chop the remaining toffees. Decorate the cakes with the toffee cream and scatter the chopped toffees over the top.

Per bar 301 kcals, **protein** 3.2g, **carbohydrate** 30.2g, **fat** 18.5g, **saturated fat** 10.9g, **fibre** 0.5g, **salt** 0.5g

Raspberry and white chocolate blondies

50 minutes, plus cooling | makes 15 | easy

200g unsalted butter, plus
extra for greasing
150g white chocolate,
roughly chopped
300g light muscovado
sugar
3 large eggs
200g plain flour
¼ tsp salt
1 tsp vanilla extract
125g raspberries

Cooking the butter until nutty and golden gives these blondies the edge before they've even made it to the oven.

Heat oven to 180°C/Fan 160°C/Gas 4. Butter, then line, a shallow rectangular tin, approximately 25 x 22cm. Melt the butter in a pan, then cook gently for about 5 minutes, until the white solids turn golden and the butter smells biscuity and sweet. Cool for 5 minutes, then add half the white chocolate and set aside for a couple of minutes to melt. Stir until smooth.

Use electric beaters to whisk the muscovado sugar and eggs together for about 2 minutes until thick and pale. Tip in the flour, salt, cooled chocolatey butter and vanilla, then fold in with a metal spoon or spatula until even.

Pour the mix into the tin, then evenly scatter over the rest of the chocolate and the raspberries. Bake for 40–45 minutes or until risen all over, with a dark golden crust. Cool completely in the tin, then cut into squares.

Per square 296 kcals, **protein** 3.7g, **carbohydrate** 37g, **fat** 15.8g, **saturated fat** 9.3g, **fibre** 0.6g, **salt** 0.2g

Black Forest brownies

1 hour | makes 20 | easy

200g butter, plus extra for greasing
225g light soft brown sugar
200g golden caster sugar
125g cocoa powder, plus extra for dusting (optional)
100g dark chocolate, broken into chunks
½ tsp salt
2 tbsp kirsch (or cherry liqueur)
4 eggs
125g self-raising flour
250g cherries, stoned, plus extra to serve (optional)

To serve (optional)
300ml whipping cream
2 tbsp kirsch
3 tbsp icing sugar, sifted, plus extra for dusting

This brownie-Black Forest gâteau mash-up is boozy, cherry-studded, chocolaty heaven. Add a big dollop of kirsch-spiked cream.

Heat the oven to 170°C/Fan 150°C/Gas 3. Butter a 20 x 30cm baking tin and line with non-stick baking paper. Put the butter, sugars, cocoa powder and chocolate in a big saucepan and melt together gently, stirring occasionally.

When everything is melted and smooth, remove from the heat for 5 minutes, then, using a wooden spoon, beat in the salt, kirsch and eggs until smooth again. Stir through the flour and cherries, then scrape into the prepared tin and bake for 30 minutes.

While the brownies are baking, prepare a roasting tin of iced water that will fit the brownie tin inside. When the brownies have a crisp top and only a slight wobble to the centre, lift the tin from the oven into the water bath – this will allow the brownies set while keeping the centre soft. Cool completely in the water.

To serve, cut the brownies into 20 squares, then whisk the whipping cream with the kirsch and icing sugar until softly peaked. Dust each brownie with a little more icing sugar and cocoa if you like, and add a dollop of kirsch cream with extra fresh cherries.

Per square 257 kcals, **protein** 3.8g, **carbohydrate** 30g, **fat** 12.7g, **saturated fat** 7.4g, **fibre** 1.8g, **salt** 0.5g

Sticky toffee squares

1 hour 15 minutes, plus cooling | makes 16 | easy

4 tbsp dulce de leche or
    ready-made caramel
175g butter, softened
150g light muscovado
    sugar
175g self-raising flour
½ tsp baking powder
2 tbsp ground almonds
3 eggs

For the toffee icing
150g butter, softened
200g golden icing sugar
4 tbsp dulce de leche or
    ready-made caramel
a large pinch of salt flakes
a drop of milk (optional)

This upside-down toffee cake has toffee icing too, but you can also make the cake and serve it as it is, or serve warm as a pudding.

Heat the oven to 180°C/Fan 160°C/Gas 4. Spread the dulce de leche into the base of a 23cm square tin lined with baking paper. Beat the butter and sugar together until soft, and in a separate bowl sift the flour and baking powder together and stir in the almonds. Beat the flour mixture into the sugar and butter in three batches, adding an egg each time. Beat the mixture until smooth then spoon it into the tin and level the top. Bake for 30 minutes or until a skewer comes out clean.

Cool for 5 minutes then invert the cake onto a wire rack and peel off the paper – don't worry if a little caramel sticks to the paper, scrape it off and add it to the top of the cake.

To make the icing, beat the butter until it's very soft and then begin to beat in the icing sugar. When half of it has been incorporated, beat in the dulce de leche, the remaining icing sugar and the salt flakes. Add a drop of milk if the icing is stiff; it needs to be light enough to spread easily. Ice the top of the cake and cut it into 16 neat squares.

Per square 439 kcals, **protein** 4.3g, **carbohydrate** 47.4g, **fat** 26g, **saturated fat** 15.1g, **fibre** 0.6g, **salt** 0.7g

Mint choc chip brownies

1 hour, plus cooling | makes 12 | easy

100g unsalted butter, chopped

200g dark chocolate, chopped (an ordinary dark chocolate works best, not a 70% one)

4 eggs

250g golden caster sugar

100g plain flour

1 tsp baking powder

30g cocoa powder

151g box Matchmakers, roughly chopped

For the icing

100g dark chocolate

50g icing sugar

peppermint essence

Think of these as a bumper version of an after-dinner mint. No pudding required if you serve these with coffee.

Heat the oven to 180°C/Fan 160°C/Gas 4. Line a 22cm square brownie tin with non-stick baking paper. Melt the butter and chocolate together in a microwave or in a heatproof bowl set over a pan of simmering water, making sure the base of the bowl does not touch the water, then leave to cool.

Whisk the eggs and sugar until light and fluffy, then fold in the cooled chocolate mixture and sift in the flour, baking powder and cocoa. Fold this in, along with the Matchmakers, to give a fudgy batter. Spoon the mixture into the tin, level the surface and bake for 25–30 minutes, or until the top is cracked but the middle is just set. Leave to cool completely.

To make the icing, melt the chocolate in a microwave or in a bowl set over a pan of simmering water, making sure the base of the bowl does not touch the water, cool a little and then drizzle over the brownies. Leave to set. Mix the icing sugar with a drop of peppermint essence and enough water to make it pourable, then drizzle it over the brownies. Cut the cake into 12 squares.

Per square 411 kcals, **protein** 5g, **carbohydrate** 54g, **fat** 19g, **saturated fat** 11g, **fibre** 1.5g, **salt** 0.4g

Peanut butter and caramel brownies

1 hour 15 minutes, plus chilling and cooling | makes 16 | a little effort

125g unsalted butter, plus
    extra for greasing
200g dark chocolate
200g golden caster sugar
1 tbsp water
3 large eggs, beaten
1 tsp vanilla extract
125g plain flour
1 tbsp cocoa powder
pinch of salt
100g salted roasted
    peanuts, roughly
    chopped

For the caramel
100g white caster sugar
100ml double cream
15g unsalted butter
½ tsp vanilla bean paste
    or extract
½ tsp sea salt flakes

**For the peanut
cheesecake**
150g full-fat soft cheese
50g golden caster sugar
75g chunky peanut butter
    (preferably unsweetened)
1 large egg
1 tsp vanilla extract

Moreish brownies with a peanut cheesecake and caramel drizzle. Keep them in the fridge – they'll last longer and have a better texture.

Butter a 23cm square baking tin and line the base and sides with non-stick baking paper. To make the caramel, tip the caster sugar into a small pan with the water and heat gently until the sugar has dissolved. Bring to the boil and cook until it is a deep amber-coloured caramel. Slowly and gradually add the double cream, stirring constantly. Add the butter and vanilla, stir to combine, then return the pan to a medium heat and continue to cook for another couple of minutes until the caramel is thick enough to coat the back of a spoon. Pour the caramel into a bowl, stir in the sea salt and cool. Chill for an hour until thickened.

To make the peanut cheesecake, beat the soft cheese, sugar and peanut butter together until smooth. Add the egg and vanilla and mix until combined. Heat the oven to 160°C/Fan 140°C/Gas 3. To make the brownie, melt the chocolate and butter in a heatproof bowl either over a pan of barely simmering water or in short bursts in the microwave. Stir until smooth and leave to cool slightly. Add the caster sugar, eggs and vanilla and beat until silky smooth. Sift the flour, cocoa and a pinch of salt into the bowl and mix again until combined.

Spread half of the brownie mixture into the tin, drizzle with all but 1 tablespoon of the salted caramel and scatter with two-thirds of the peanuts. Carefully spoon over the remaining brownie mixture. Spoon the peanut cheesecake mixture in random dollops over the top of the brownie and lightly swirl through the brownie mix with a knife or the handle of a spoon. Scatter with the remaining peanuts and drizzle over the remaining 1 tablespoon of caramel.

Bake for 30 minutes until the brownie has set and slightly risen at the edges. It will still be slightly soft in the middle. Leave to cool completely before chilling in the fridge and cutting into 16 small squares to serve.

Per brownie 404 kcals, **protein** 7g, **carbohydrate** 33.6g, **fat** 26g, **saturated fat** 13g, **fibre** 2.3g, **salt** 0.5g

Rosemary and demerara shortbread

45 minutes, plus chilling | makes about 15 | easy

50g golden caster sugar

2–3 tsp rosemary needles

100g unsalted butter,
   very soft

1 tbsp semolina or rice
   flour

140g plain flour, sifted

demerara sugar, for dusting

A new take on the classic favourite, this shortbread is quick and easy baking and will please a crowd.

Put the caster sugar in a food processor with the rosemary needles and whizz until the rosemary is finely chopped. Add the butter and whizz, then add the semolina or rice flour followed by the flour, bit by bit, until the mix comes together as a dough. Turn out onto some baking paper, roll into a log about 4cm across, then wrap in cling film and chill for 30 minutes.

Heat the oven to 200°C/Fan 180°C/Gas 6. Cut the dough into 1cm thick rounds and space them well apart on a baking sheet. Sprinkle a little demerara onto each and bake for 10–15 minutes or until lightly golden. Cool for a couple of minutes on the sheet and then transfer to a wire rack to cool completely.

Per biscuit 97 kcals, **protein** 1g, **carbohydrate** 11.4g, **fat** 5.6g, **saturated fat** 3.5g, **fibre** 0.3g, **salt** 0g

Pistachio fancies

50 minutes | makes 16 | a little effort

100g pistachio kernels

150g golden caster sugar

150g butter, at room
    temperature

3 eggs

150g self-raising flour

2 tbsp milk

8–12 white chocolate balls,
    such as Lindt balls, split
    in half

For the icing

250g fondant icing sugar,
    plus a little extra for the
    green icing

green food colouring

**These cakes have a lovely green colour and the pistachios help to
keep them deliciously moist for several days (if you can resist them!).**

Heat the oven to 190°C/Fan 170°C/Gas 5. Line a 21cm square tin with
non-stick baking paper. Whizz the pistachios in a food processor, add the
sugar and whizz again. Add the butter and pulse until smooth then add the
eggs and flour and process to a smooth batter. Add a splash of milk if you
need to, the cake mix should drop easily off a spoon. Pour the mixture into
the tin and bake for 20 minutes or until risen and lightly browned. Cool for
15 minutes then turn the cake out of the tin and leave to cool completely.

Trim the edge and cut the cake into 16 squares. Put a halved Lindt ball
flat-side down on each, then put each square in a fairy cake case.

Mix the fondant icing sugar with some water until you have a smooth, just
spoonable icing. You want it to coat the cakes but not run off too easily.
Spoon most of the icing over the cakes, coating the top and Lindt balls
and letting it run down the sides into the cases. Mix the remaining icing
with a little more icing sugar and a tiny amount of green food colouring.
Drizzle this back and forth across the surface of each. Leave to set.

Per square 276 kcals, **protein** 3.8g, **carbohydrate** 35.2g, **fat** 13.3g, **saturated fat** 6.5g, **fibre** 1g, **salt** 0.3g

Fresh cherry and coconut lamingtons

2 hours 15 minutes, plus cooling | makes 9 | easy

100g unsalted butter,
  melted, plus extra for
  greasing
200g cherries
250g plain flour
50g cornflour
2 tsp baking powder
pinch of salt
150g full-fat coconut
  yoghurt or Greek yoghurt
50ml sunflower oil
250g golden caster sugar
2 tsp vanilla extract
3 medium eggs, plus
  1 egg yolk

For the decoration
a jar of cherry jam
100g desiccated or
  shredded coconut

Lamingtons, originally from Australia, make a delicious teatime treat. This version is decorated in cherry jam and desiccated coconut, topped with a fresh cherry.

Heat the oven to 170°C/Fan 150°C/Gas 3½. Butter a 20cm deep, square cake tin and line the base with non-stick baking paper. Set aside 9 cherries, then stone and finely dice the rest and leave them in a sieve while you make the batter.

Sift together the flours, baking powder and a good pinch of salt, then set aside 2 tablespoons of this mix.

Beat the butter, yoghurt, oil, sugar and vanilla in a big mixing bowl until smooth. Add the eggs and yolk, one at a time, beating in between each addition. Beat in the flour mixture, then toss the diced cherries with the reserved 2 tablespoons of flour, mix to coat them, and then fold these in. Scrape the mixture into the tin and bake for 50–55 minutes until a skewer poked in the centre comes out clean. Cover the tin with foil and cool the cake completely (this helps to keep the sponge from drying out).

Turn the cake out onto a tray and freeze for 30 minutes to firm it up. Trim the edges to make them even and straight, then divide the cake into 9 squares.

Heat the jam in a pan or microwave until hot, then use a sieve to drain into a bowl. Spread the coconut on a plate and dunk each cake first into the jam to coat all sides (except the bottom), then the coconut (stick a fork into the base to help). Top each with a cherry and leave for an hour to set and defrost fully.

Per square 582 kcals, **protein** 6.8g, **carbohydrate** 80.9g, **fat** 26.1g, **saturated fat** 14.2g, **fibre** 3.5g, **salt** 0.6g

Raspberry and white chocolate macaroons

50 minutes | makes 50 | a little effort

275g icing sugar
120g ground almonds
8g sachet of powdered egg
    white (look in the baking
    section)
85g egg whites (about
    2–3 eggs)
pink food colouring
3 tbsp seedless raspberry
    jam

For the ganache
75g white chocolate
15g butter
75ml double cream

A perfectly indulgent macaroon filled with white chocolate ganache. Filled macaroons will keep in an airtight container for up to 12 hours, so are perfect little treats to make ahead.

To make the ganache, melt the chocolate and butter together in a microwave or in a bowl set over simmering water, making sure the base of the bowl does not touch the water. Leave to cool. Lightly whip the cream and fold in. Cover and set aside. Line two baking sheets with non-stick baking paper and heat the oven to 160°C/Fan 140°C/Gas 3.

Sift the icing sugar and almonds into a bowl. Use a food processor to re-grind any almond left in the sieve to a fine powder and add to the rest.

Whisk the powdered egg white and fresh egg whites together to form stiff peaks. Add the colouring, a tiny amount at a time, and whisk. You're after a soft pink colour.

Fold the almond mixture in – the volume will decrease massively. Transfer the mixture to a piping bag or a plastic food bag with the corner snipped off and pipe rounds of the mixture onto the baking sheets. They will spread a little as you pipe but each macaroon should be about 5cm in diameter.

Cook for about 12–15 minutes, until risen with a frilly base but not coloured. Watch them and if they start to turn golden, reduce the oven temperature. Carefully loosen each macaroon. If they stick to the baking sheets, pour a little water under the baking paper, being careful not to get the macaroons wet, and leave for a minute to steam them off from underneath (or, if you have the space, place the baking sheet in the freezer for a few minutes). Leave to cool.

Spread a macaroon with a little ganache and another with raspberry jam. Sandwich together and leave for 15 minutes for the fillings to soften the macaroons slightly, then serve.

Per macaroon 115 kcals, **protein** 1.9g, **carbohydrate** 14.9g, **fat** 5.7g, **saturated fat** 2g, **fibre** 0.4g, **salt** 0.06g

Black Forest cupcakes

1 hour, plus cooling | makes 12 | a little effort

40g cocoa powder

100ml boiling water

150g unsalted butter, softened

175g golden caster sugar

3 medium eggs, beaten

1 tsp vanilla extract

150g plain flour

2 tsp baking powder

½ tsp bicarbonate of soda

pinch of salt

2 tbsp soured cream, at room temperature

For the buttercream

200g 70% dark chocolate, chopped

175g golden caster sugar

3 medium egg whites

pinch of salt

225g unsalted butter, softened

For the decoration

2 tbsp cherry brandy or kirsch

4 tbsp morello cherry jam

12 natural glacé or morello cherries

Cherries, kirsch and dark chocolate make an indulgent, grown-up cupcake.

Line a 12-hole muffin tin with paper cases and heat the oven to 180°C/Fan 160°C/Gas 4. Tip the cocoa into a small bowl, add the boiling water and whisk until smooth. Leave to cool.

Cream the butter and caster sugar together with electric beaters until really pale, light and fluffy. Gradually add the beaten eggs, mixing well in between each addition and scraping down the sides of the bowl from time to time with a rubber spatula. Add the vanilla extract and cocoa mixture and mix again until thoroughly combined.

Sift the flour, baking powder, bicarbonate of soda and a pinch of salt into the bowl, add the soured cream and fold in using a rubber spatula or large metal spoon. Mix until smooth and then divide the mixture evenly between the paper cases. Bake in the oven for about 20 minutes or until well risen and a wooden skewer inserted into the middle of the cakes comes out clean. Leave the cakes to rest in the tin for 3–4 minutes and then transfer them to a wire rack to cool until completely cold.

Meanwhile, make the chocolate meringue buttercream. Melt the chocolate in a heatproof bowl either set over a pan of barely simmering water or in the microwave on a low setting, stirring until smooth. Put the sugar, egg whites and a pinch of salt in a medium-sized, heatproof bowl that will fit snugly over (but not touch) a pan of simmering water. Whisk until the sugar has completely dissolved and the mixture is foamy. Continue to cook until the mixture is hot to the touch, thickens enough to only just hold a ribbon trail and turns from opaque to bright glossy white.

Quickly scoop the meringue mixture into the bowl of the mixer with a whisk and beat on a medium-high speed for about 3 minutes until the mixture has doubled in volume and is thick, stiff, glossy and cold (or scoop it into a new bowl and beat with hand beaters for a little longer).

Gradually add the butter to the cooled meringue mixture, beating constantly on a low-medium speed, until the buttercream is smooth, thick and spreadable. If it starts to curdle, continue whisking and it will be smooth again after a minute or so. Fold in the melted chocolate.

Using a teaspoon scoop out a hole from the top of each cupcake (you can eat this bit if you like), brush the cakes with cherry brandy and fill the holes with cherry jam. Spread the chocolate buttercream generously over the top of each cake and finish with a glacé or morello cherry.

Per serving 536 kcals, **protein** 5.1g **carbohydrate** 55.2g, **fat** 32.6g, **saturated fat** 20g, **fibre** 1.7g, **salt** 0.6g

Blackberry and chocolate cakes

1 hour, plus cooling | makes 12 | easy

175g butter

100g 72% (or above) dark chocolate, finely chopped

300g plain flour

375g golden caster sugar

25g good-quality cocoa powder

1 tsp bicarbonate of soda

pinch of salt

2 eggs

200ml red wine

100ml boiling water

200g punnet of blackberries

150g butter, softened

300g icing sugar

With a berry velvet cake and buttercream icing, these cupcakes are almost too pretty to eat.

Heat the oven to 180°C/Fan 160°C/Gas 4. Put the butter and chocolate in a small pan and melt, stirring, until smooth.

Mix the flour, sugar, cocoa and bicarbonate of soda with a pinch of salt in a mixing bowl. Whisk the eggs and wine together. Add the chocolate and egg mixtures to the dry ingredients, then pour in the boiling water and whisk until the cake batter is smooth. Divide the mixture between 12 large muffin cases. Drop 2 or 3 blackberries into the top of each one. Bake for 35 minutes or until cooked through. Cool on a wire rack.

Whizz the remaining blackberries to a purée and push through a sieve. Beat the butter until very soft then beat in half of the icing sugar. Beat in about 6 tablespoons of the purée, followed by the remaining sugar, and spoon into a piping bag. Pipe the blackberry buttercream onto the cakes.

Per serving 597 kcals, **protein** 4.9g, **carbohydrate** 77.9g, **fat** 27.6g, **saturated fat** 16.7g, **fibre** 3.7g, **salt** 0.8g

Lemon and blueberry cupcakes with meringue frosting

1 hour, plus cooling | makes 12 | a little effort

150g unsalted butter,
  softened
150g golden or white
  caster sugar
3 medium eggs
finely grated zest and juice
  of 1 unwaxed lemon
175g plain flour
25g cornflour
2 level tsp baking powder
pinch of salt
blueberry preserve or jam,
  to fill
12 blueberries, to decorate

For the frosting
3 medium egg whites
175g white caster sugar
pinch of salt
1 tbsp water

These cupcakes are light, fluffy and not overly sweet – perfect for a summer's day. If you don't want to use meringue, try a simple buttercream icing with a tablespoon of fresh lemon juice instead.

Heat the oven to 180°C/Fan 160°C/Gas 4. Cream the butter and caster sugar with electric beaters until very pale and light.

Gradually add the eggs, mixing well in between each addition and scraping down the sides of the bowl. Add the zest from the lemons and mix again. Sift the flour, cornflour, baking powder and a pinch of salt into the bowl, add the juice from 1 lemon and mix again until the batter is silky smooth.

Divide the mixture between muffin tins lined with 12 paper cases and bake for about 20 minutes until well risen, golden and a wooden skewer comes out clean from the middle of the cakes. Cool in the tin for 3–4 minutes and then transfer to a wire rack until cold.

Use a small sharp knife to cut a deep cone from the top of each cake and slice off the pointed end of each cone. Spoon 1 teaspoon of the blueberry preserve into each cake and replace the cake 'lids'.

To make the frosting, put the egg whites, sugar, pinch of salt and water in a medium heatproof bowl. Set the bowl over a pan of gently simmering water and whisk constantly to dissolve the sugar and cook the egg whites into a meringue cloud that is hot to the touch and will hold a ribbon trail – this will take about 4 minutes.

Quickly scoop the mixture into the bowl of a free-standing mixer fitted with a whisk attachment and whisk on a medium-high speed for a further 3–4 minutes until the meringue becomes stiff and glossy. Spoon the meringue into a large piping bag fitted with a large star nozzle. Pipe generous swirls on top of each cake and leave to set for 20 minutes. Toast the meringue frosting using a blowtorch. Top with blueberries.

Per cupcake 285 kcals, **protein** 3.7g, **carbohydrate** 41.8g, **fat** 11.6g, **saturated fat** 6.8g, **fibre** 0.7g, **salt** 0.4g

Coffee and walnut cupcakes

40 minutes, plus cooling | makes 12 | easy

100g walnuts

140g golden caster sugar

3 tbsp milk, heated

2 tsp instant coffee
granules

100g salted butter,
softened

2 tbsp walnut oil

2 eggs

75g self-raising flour

75g plain wholemeal flour

½ tsp bicarbonate of soda

For the icing

350g unsalted butter,
softened

400g icing sugar

2 tbsp cocoa powder

2 tbsp instant coffee
granules dissolved in
4 tbsp boiling water

1 tsp vanilla extract

There's no need for after-dinner coffees with these cupcakes. Pipe the icing sky-high for maximum cake drama.

Heat the oven to 180°C/Fan 160°C/Gas 4 and line a 12-hole muffin tin with muffin cases. Put the walnuts in a food processor with about half the sugar and whizz until very finely chopped (like ground almonds).

Mix the milk and coffee to dissolve the coffee (if it needs some help, pop it in the microwave for a few seconds).

Tip the walnut-sugar mix, remaining sugar, milky coffee, softened butter, oil, eggs, flours and bicarb into a large mixing bowl and beat with an electric whisk until smooth. Divide the mixture between the muffin cases then bake for 18 minutes, or until golden and risen, and a skewer poked into the centre comes out clean. Cool for 5 minutes in the tin, then lift the cakes onto a wire rack to cool completely.

For the icing, put the butter in a big mixing bowl and beat for about 5 minutes until very pale and creamy. Sift in the icing sugar and cocoa then add the coffee and vanilla and beat for another 3–5 minutes until very fluffy.

To decorate, put the icing into a large piping bag fitted with a star nozzle and pipe swirls of icing on top of each cake, then leave to set for 20 minutes before serving.

Per cupcake 598 kcals, **protein** 4.7g, **carbohydrate** 55.2g, **fat** 39.4g, **saturated fat** 20.5g, **fibre** 1.7g, **salt** 0.4g

Party cupcakes

1 hour, plus cooling | makes 24 cakes | easy

175g butter
175g golden caster sugar
175g self-raising flour
3 eggs
½ tsp vanilla extract
1 tbsp cocoa
3 tbsp milk
75g shelled pistachios, ground
zest of 1 lemon

For the icing

3 tbsp lemon juice (use the zested lemon, above)
400g icing sugar
food colouring (we used yellow)
150g white chocolate
2 tbsp milk
2 tsp shelled pistachios, chopped
150g butter, softened
2 tbsp cocoa powder

Making one cupcake mixture and flavouring it three ways is a simple, show-off way to make a party pud.

Put 24 cupcake cases into 2 x 12-hole tins. Heat the oven to 180°C/Fan 160°C/Gas 4. Beat the butter and sugar until fluffy and then beat in the flour, eggs and vanilla. Working quickly, divide the mix into three. Beat the cocoa and 1 tablespoon of the milk into 1 batch, the pistachios and remaining milk into the next and the lemon zest into the last.

Divide each batch between 8 cases and bake for 12–15 minutes, or until risen. Swap the trays around halfway through cooking if you need to. Leave to cool.

Mix the lemon juice gradually into half the icing sugar to make the lemon icing. Take out 2 tablespoons, colour it with food colouring, then put it in a piping bag. Top each lemon cake with white icing and allow to set. Snip the corner off the bag of coloured icing and pipe a cross hatch or dots on each.

For the pistachio icing, gently melt the white chocolate with the milk in a pan and stir until smooth. Allow to thicken, then spread it onto each pistachio cake. Sprinkle with pistachios.

For the chocolate icing, beat the butter with the remaining sugar and cocoa, spoon into a piping bag with a star nozzle and pipe onto the chocolate cakes.

Per cupcake 291 kcals, **protein** 3.3g, **carbohydrate** 32.6g, **fat** 16.3g, **saturated fat** 9g, **fibre** 0.7g, **salt** 0.4g

Sour cherry cakes with cream cheese frosting

1½ hours, plus soaking | makes 16 | easy

400g tinned or preserved cherries in juice (make sure they are pitted)
100g dried sour cherries, chopped
250g butter, softened
180g golden caster sugar
4 eggs
175g plain flour
75g ground almonds
1 tsp baking powder

For the frosting
150g butter, softened
150g soft cheese
225g icing sugar

A seasonal favourite. The cream cheese frosting tones down the tartness of the cherries.

Drain the juice from the tinned or preserved cherries into a bowl, add the dried sour cherry pieces and leave them to soak for 30 minutes. Roughly chop the tinned/preserved cherries, reserving 8 whole ones.

Heat the oven to 200°C/Fan 180°C/Gas 6. Beat the butter and sugar together until they are light and fluffy, then beat in the eggs one at a time, followed by the flour, almonds and baking powder. Drain the sour cherry pieces (keeping the juice) and stir these in, followed by the chopped cherries.

Divide the mix between 16 muffin holes lined with muffin cases or squares of non-stick baking paper. Bake for 25 minutes until they are risen and golden on top, then leave to cool.

To make the syrup, put the remaining juice in a pan and bubble until you have thick syrup. To make the frosting, beat the butter, then beat in the soft cheese until smooth, followed by the icing sugar (if it gets too warm at this point just chill it in the fridge until it thickens).

Spoon the frosting into a piping bag fitted with a star nozzle. Poke a thick skewer or skinny end of a spoon carefully down one side of the bag to make a trough and pour the cherry syrup inside. Pipe the frosting onto the cakes in a swirl and finish the top of each with half a cherry.

Per cake 435 kcals, **protein** 4.8g, **carbohydrate** 42.2g, **fat** 27.7g, **saturated fat** 15.6g, **fibre** 1.1g, **salt** 0.6g

Cakes for pudding

Amalfi lemon drizzle cake

2 hours 15 minutes, plus cooling | serves 12 | easy

2 Amalfi lemons
175g golden caster sugar
175g butter, softened, plus
    extra for greasing
175g self-raising flour
50g ground almonds
1 tsp baking powder
3 large eggs

For the candied peel

1 Amalfi lemon
100g caster sugar, plus
    extra to coat
100ml water

For the drizzle

zest of 2 Amalfi lemons,
    and 75ml of juice
100g golden granulated or
    caster sugar

Amalfi lemons from Italy have an intense aroma and flavour that makes this cake even better, but you can use regular ones too. Dress it up even further with some tart candied peel.

Put the whole lemons into a pan and cover with water. Bring to the boil and simmer for 45 minutes (topping up the water if you need to), or until the lemons pierce really easily with a knife. Drain the lemons, let them cool, then cut them into quarters, removing any pips. Whizz to a smooth purée in a food processor.

While the lemons are boiling, make the candied peels. Peel the lemon then slice it into thin strips. Heat the caster sugar with the water until the sugar has dissolved, then simmer the lemon peel until softened. Drain then immediately toss in plenty more sugar to coat and leave to dry.

Heat the oven to 160°C/Fan 140°C/Gas 3 and butter and line the base and ends of a 900g loaf tin with non-stick baking paper. Put the cooled lemon pulp, sugar, butter, flour, almonds, baking powder and eggs in a big mixing bowl and whisk together until smooth. Scrape into the tin and bake for 1 hour, or until a skewer poked into the centre comes out clean.

Cool the cake in the tin for about 20 minutes, then carefully turn it out onto a wire rack. Poke the top with a skewer a few times, then mix together the drizzle ingredients and immediately spoon over the top to coat. Scatter the candied peel over the top. Leave to cool completely, then serve in slices.

Per serving 310 kcals, **protein** 4.4g, **carbohydrate** 36.7g, **fat** 1.1g, **saturated fat** 8.2g, **fibre** 1.1g, **salt** 0.5g

Strawberry and Earl Grey roulade

1 hour 10 minutes, plus cooling and resting | serves 8–10 | easy

3 tbsp lemon juice

2 tbsp loose leaf Earl
Grey tea

4 eggs, separated

75g caster sugar, plus extra
for sprinkling

75g plain flour

2 tbsp sunflower oil

a few drops of orange
extract

For the filling

300ml whipping cream

2 tbsp lemon juice

3 tbsp icing sugar

15 medium-large
strawberries

This light-as-air Swiss roll is a real showstopper. By double-flipping the sponge, you end up with the delicate pale underside on the outside – a trick taken from Japanese baking.

Heat the oven to 180°C/Fan 160°C/Gas 4 and line the base of a 25 x 35cm Swiss roll tin or shallow baking tray with non-stick baking paper. Mix the lemon juice with 1 tablespoon of the tea and warm until piping hot (in a mug in a microwave is easiest). Leave for a few minutes, stirring every so often to draw out as much flavour as possible. Strain through a sieve.

Crush the remaining tea with a pestle and mortar (or whizz with the flour in a food processor to break it up). Beat the egg yolks with 25g of the sugar until pale and frothy, then mix the flour, oil, remaining crushed tea leaves and the tea-infused lemon juice. Stir in the orange extract. Clean the beaters and beat the egg whites in another bowl to soft peaks. Add the remaining sugar and continue beating until thick and glossy. Gently fold the meringue mixture into the cake mixture in thirds until most streaks of egg white have disappeared. Spread into the tin as smoothly as you can and bake for about 13–15 minutes.

Lay a large sheet of baking paper on your work surface and flip the cake onto it. Peel off the baking paper, then flip the cake a second time onto a new sheet of baking paper dusted liberally with caster sugar so the cake is now sitting the way it was baked. Roll up the cake from one of the longest edges with the paper, and leave to cool.

Once completely cool, carefully unroll the cake. Make the filling by beating the cream with the lemon juice and icing sugar until it is just holding its shape. Trim the tops and bottoms of the strawberries so they can sandwich together in an even line along the length of the cake. Spread a thin layer of cream on the cake, then line up the strawberries along the inside edge. Roll the cake again from the strawberry-lined edge so you have the strawberries sitting in the centre. Chill for 2 hours before neatly slicing to serve.

Per serving 245 kcal, **protein** 4g, **carbohydrate** 20g, **fat** 16.6g, **saturated fat** 8.5g, **fibre** 0.6g, **salt** 0.1g

Banana loaf with passion fruit frosting

1½ hours | serves 10 | easy

75g butter, softened, plus
  extra for greasing
110g soft brown sugar
125g plain flour
75g wholemeal flour
2 tsp baking powder
2 eggs
4 very ripe bananas,
  mashed
75g pecans, each snapped
  in half

For the frosting
75g butter
75g cream cheese
3 passion fruit
150g icing sugar

Our take on the ever-popular banana loaf. Made with pecans and a tropical passion fruit frosting, this is a teatime treat to share with family and friends.

Heat the oven to 180°C/Fan 160°C/Gas 4. Beat the butter, sugar, flours, baking powder, eggs and banana together. Stir in the nuts and spoon the mixture into a greased and lined 450g loaf tin. Bake for 1–1½ hours or until a skewer comes out clean. Cool for 10 minutes in the tin then lift out and cool on a wire rack.

To make the frosting, beat the butter until soft, then beat in the cream cheese. Halve the passion fruit and scoop the seeds and pulp into a sieve set over a bowl. Stir the pulp until all the juices have been pushed through. Add the sugar and 2 tablespoons of passion fruit juice to the butter and cream cheese and stir to combine. Spread the frosting over the top of the loaf and drizzle over the remaining juice. Top with the passion fruit seeds if you like.

Per serving 428 kcal, **protein** 5.2g, **carbohydrate** 49.4g, **fat** 22.7g, **saturated fat** 10.9g, **fibre** 2.5g, **salt** 0.6g

Orange and dark chocolate cake with spiced syrup

2½ hours | serves 8–10 | easy

2 thin-skinned oranges,
  cleaned
50g dark chocolate
200g unsalted butter,
  softened, plus extra
  for greasing
225g golden caster sugar
3 large eggs
150g plain flour
2 level tsp baking powder
½ tsp ground cinnamon
125g ground almonds
pinch of salt

For the syrup
2 oranges
juice of ½ lemon
125g golden caster sugar
1 cinnamon stick
6 cardamom pods, bruised
  and seeds lightly crushed
2 tbsp water

Don't be fooled by the length of this recipe, this cake is very easy to make.

To make the cake, put the oranges in a pan and cover with water. Bring to the boil, half cover with a lid and simmer gently for about 1 hour or until tender, topping up with more boiling water as necessary. Drain and cool.

Heat the oven to 160°C/Fan 140°C/Gas 3. Grease and line the base and ends of a large 900g loaf tin with a strip of greased baking paper. Cut the cooked oranges into quarters and slice out the pithy core, stalk end and any seeds. Roughly chop the quarters, tip them into a food processor and whizz until almost smooth but still retaining some small pieces of peel.

Grate the chocolate using the coarse side of a box grater. Cream the butter and caster sugar with electric beaters until really pale and light. Gradually add the eggs, mixing well in between each addition and scraping down the sides of the bowl from time to time. Sift the plain flour, baking powder and cinnamon into the bowl, add the ground almonds and a pinch of salt and mix again. Add the whizzed oranges and grated chocolate then mix until smooth.

Spoon the mixture into the tin, spread to level the surface and bake for 1–1½ hours or until golden brown, well-risen and a wooden skewer inserted into the middle of the cake comes out clean. Leave the cake to rest in the tin for 10 minutes then turn out onto a cooling rack.

To make the syrup, remove the peel from the oranges in strips using a vegetable peeler. Slice the peel into fine shreds and blanch these in boiling water for 1 minute. Squeeze the juice from the oranges and pour it into a small pan with the lemon juice. Add the caster sugar, cinnamon stick, cardamom pods and water. Bring to the boil and simmer until reduced by half and thickened to a pourable syrup. Add the blanched orange peels and simmer for a further 30 seconds. Cool a little.

Carefully and slowly spoon the syrup and orange peels over the cake and serve with any extra alongside.

Per serving 489 kcals, **protein** 7.4g, **carbohydrate** 53.5g, **fat** 27.3g, **saturated fat** 12.5g, **fibre** 2.5g, **salt** 0.3g

Cherry Bakewell tart

1¼ hours, plus chilling | serves 8 | easy

375g bought sweet pastry
100g butter, softened
100g golden caster sugar
3 eggs (2 whole plus
  1 yolk) beaten
100g ground almonds
1 tsp almond extract
50g self-raising flour
1 tsp baking powder
5 tbsp seedless raspberry
  jam, warmed in a pan
175g icing sugar
10 glacé cherries, halved,
  to decorate

Our classic cherry tart is exceedingly good – serve with a cup of builder's tea for a proper English teatime treat.

Heat the oven to 180°C/Fan 160°C/Gas 4. Roll out the pastry to 20p coin thickness then use it to line a long rectangular tart tin, approximately 35 x 12cm, or a round tin of about 23cm. Line with non-stick baking paper then fill with baking beans. Chill in the fridge for 20 minutes. Bake for 15 minutes then take out the paper and beans and cook for another 5 minutes until the pastry is sandy coloured and cooked. Take it out of the oven.

Beat the butter and sugar together then gradually beat in the eggs and egg yolk. Mix in the ground almonds and almond extract, then sift in the self-raising flour and baking powder and fold them in.

Spread a thin layer of jam over the base of the pastry. Spoon over the almond mix then level out. Bake on a lower shelf for 30–40 minutes until set.

Mix the icing sugar with just enough water until it coats the back of a spoon (about 1 tablespoon). Spread a layer of icing over the top of the tart, going right up to the pastry edge, then leave to set. Decorate with cherries.

Per serving 613 kcals, **protein** 7.9g, **carbohydrate** 72.7g, **fat** 34.3g, **saturated fat** 12.6g, **fibre** 2g, **salt** 0.75g

Caramel chip banana cake

1½ hours, plus cooling | serves 8 | easy

175g butter, very soft
150g golden caster sugar
2 very ripe bananas,
   roughly chopped
3 eggs
140g self-raising flour
75g ground almonds
½ tsp baking powder
3 tbsp natural yoghurt

For the caramel chips
200g golden caster sugar

For the frosting
150g butter, very soft
100g icing sugar, sifted

This cake is brilliantly useful for using up bananas that are slightly past their best. The caramel gives a bit of a twist to your classic banana loaf too.

Heat your oven to 160°C/ Fan 140°C/Gas 3. Butter and line a 900g loaf tin with a strip of baking parchment that hangs over the short ends.

To make the caramel chips, tip the sugar into a frying pan, shaking it to an even layer. Heat gently until it melts, tipping the pan to make sure the edges don't burn. Once melted to a golden caramel, pour it onto a baking sheet set on something that won't burn or melt. Leave to cool, then smash it into small pieces.

Beat the butter and sugar with an electric whisk until light and fluffy. Add the bananas and beat in with the eggs, flour, almonds, baking powder and yoghurt until smooth. Stir in one-third of the caramel and spoon the mixture into the tin. Bake for 45–50 minutes until the cake is golden and a skewer comes out clean. Cool in the tin, then lift out by the parchment ends.

Make the frosting by beating the butter and sugar together. Choose a few pieces of caramel for decoration and crush the rest finely. Stir the crushed caramel into the frosting, ice the cake and decorate with caramel chips.

Per serving 702 kcals, **protein** 7.3g, **carbohydrates** 79.6g **fat** 41.6g, **saturated fat** 22.4g, **fibre** 1.5g, **salt** 1.07g

Coconut loaf with lime and lemon drizzle

1 hour 15 minutes, plus cooling | serves 8 | easy

175g unsalted butter, plus 2 tsp, softened

200g golden caster sugar, plus 5 tbsp

4 medium eggs (3 whole and 1 separated)

2 unwaxed lemons

1 unwaxed lime

175g plain flour

2 level tsp baking powder

pinch of salt

50g desiccated coconut

3 tbsp coconut milk or whole milk

2 tsp lemon curd

1–2 tbsp shredded or desiccated coconut, to finish

Lime and coconut take a traditional lemon drizzle loaf to a new level.

Heat the oven to 180°C/Fan 160°C/Gas 4. Grease and line the base and ends of a 450g loaf tin with a strip of greased baking paper. Cream 175g of the softened butter and the 200g of caster sugar together with electric beaters until pale, light and fluffy. Mix the whole eggs and the egg yolk and gradually add them to the creamed butter and sugar, mixing well in between each addition and scraping down the bowl in between.

Finely grate the zest from the lemons and lime and add the zest to the mixture. Sift the plain flour, baking powder and a pinch of salt into the bowl, add the coconut and the milk and mix gently until smooth. In a separate bowl, whisk the egg white until it will hold a peak and carefully fold it into the cake mixture using a large spoon or rubber spatula. Pour the mixture into the prepared tin and level it with the back of a spoon.

Mix the remaining butter and lemon curd together and spoon into a small freezer bag. Squeeze the mixture into one corner of the bag, snip the end off and pipe a stripe of lemony butter down the middle of the cake mixture. This will ensure that the cake rises well with a nice caramelised crack down the middle. Bake the cake in the bottom third of the oven for 45–50 minutes or until well risen, golden brown and a skewer inserted into the middle of the cake comes out clean. Loosely cover the top of the cake with a sheet of baking paper if it is starting to brown too much.

While the cake is baking, make the lemon and lime syrup. Squeeze the juice from both lemons and the lime and pour the juice into a small saucepan. Add the remaining 5 tablespoons of sugar and set the pan over a low-medium heat to dissolve the sugar.

Bring the juice to the boil and reduce it by half. Leave the cooked cake to cool in the tin for 2–3 minutes and then prick it all over with a wooden skewer. Brush or spoon the warm syrup over the cake, scatter with the shredded or remaining desiccated coconut and leave to cool in the tin.

Per serving 483 kcals, **protein** 5.8g, **carbohydrate** 55g, **fat** 27g, **saturated fat** 17.1g, **fibre** 2.4g, **salt** 0.5g

Earl Grey tea loaf with orange frosting

1 hour 20 minutes, plus infusing | serves 8 | easy

4 Earl Grey tea bags
225ml whole milk
150g golden raisins
150g sultanas
100g butter
100g light muscovado
    sugar
1 egg
225g self-raising flour
juice and zest of 1 orange

For the orange frosting
150g butter, softened
275g icing sugar
juice of 1 orange (cut some
    strips of zest for
    decoration with a zester)

Steeping your tea in milk rather than water brings out the flavour to infuse the entire bake. The orange frosting gives this loaf an extra kick.

Put the tea bags and milk in a pan and bring to just below boiling point. Take the pan off the heat and leave to infuse for 15 minutes. Put the raisins and sultanas in a bowl and pour over the tea mixture, squeezing the liquid from the bags. Cover, then leave for at least an hour.

Heat the oven to 180°C/Fan 160°C/Gas 4. Grease and line the base of a 900g loaf tin with non-stick baking paper. Beat the butter and sugar together until creamy, then beat in the egg. Fold in the flour and fruit mixture with the tea in alternate batches, then fold in the orange juice and zest. Spoon the mixture into the tin, then smooth over the surface. Bake for 1 hour or until a skewer pushed into the centre comes out clean. Leave to cool in the tin, then lift out.

To make the frosting, beat the butter with the sugar to a crumbly mixture, then beat in the orange juice until creamy. Frost the top of the cake (and sides, if you like) and leave it to set for an hour. Decorate with the orange zest.

Per serving 651 kcals, **protein** 5.5g, **carbohydrate** 93.6g, **fat** 28g, **saturated fat** 17.2g, **fibre** 2.2g, **salt** 0.8g

Coffee and walnut Swiss roll

50 minutes, plus cooling | serves 6 | a little effort

6 eggs

175g golden caster sugar, plus extra to dust

175g self-raising flour

2 tsp coffee granules mixed with a little water to form a paste

50g butter, melted

75g walnuts, toasted and chopped

icing sugar, to dust

cocoa powder, to dust

For the filling

250g mascarpone

1 tsp coffee granules, mixed with a little water to form a paste

4 tbsp golden caster sugar

150ml double cream, whipped

75g walnuts, roughly chopped

A Swiss roll is always fun to make and this grown-up version of the classic recipe is just so delicious with its coffee, walnut and creamy mascarpone filling.

Heat the oven to 200°C/Fan 180°C/Gas 6. Line a 27 x 40cm Swiss roll tin with non-stick baking paper. Whisk the eggs and sugar together until they are light and fluffy – this can take about 5 minutes, so keep going until they are really light. Fold in the flour then gradually fold in the coffee, butter and walnuts. Spoon the mix into the tin, level the surface and bake for 12–15 minutes until pale but cooked and springy in the middle.

Leave to cool a little, then turn out onto a sheet of non-stick baking paper dusted with sugar. Roll up like a Swiss roll, keeping the paper sandwiched between the cake layers, then leave to cool.

Mix the mascarpone with the coffee and sugar and fold in the cream. When the sponge is completely cool, unroll it carefully and spread with the mascarpone mix, stud with walnuts then roll up like a Swiss roll again – this time without the paper in between.

Dust with icing sugar and cocoa (we used a template to create a striped pattern, but you can use any that you like) and serve in slices.

Per serving 899 kcals, **protein** 15.5g, **carbohydrate** 69.4g, **fat** 64g, **saturated fat** 27.7g, **fibre** 1.8g, **salt** 0.71g

Double chocolate and raspberry babka

2½ hours, plus rising and proving | serves 8 | a little effort

175ml milk

1 tbsp fast-action (instant) yeast

640g strong flour, plus extra for dusting

100g golden caster sugar

1 tsp salt

1 tbsp vanilla

275g butter, softened

2 egg yolks

100g white chocolate, chopped

2 tbsp freeze dried raspberries, crushed

For the filling

50g golden caster sugar

50g butter

75g dark chocolate

3 tbsp freeze dried raspberries, crushed

For the sugar syrup

125g golden caster sugar

125ml water

A twisted sweet bread with ribbons of raspberry and chocolate.

Put the milk, yeast and 160g of the flour in the bowl of a stand mixer and mix it to a sloppy dough. Cover and leave for several hours, somewhere warm, to activate the yeast and turn it into a bowl full of bubbly dough. Add the remaining flour, sugar, salt, vanilla, butter and egg yolks and mix with a dough hook until the mixture turns into a soft dough that leaves the side of the bowl. This can take up to 20 minutes, so you can leave it to mix and check it every few minutes.

Tip the dough out onto a floured work surface and press it out into a long rectangle about 1cm thick. Scatter over half of the chocolate and raspberries, fold the dough in half widthways and scatter over the remaining raspberries and chocolate, fold the side of the dough over the filling and pinch the edges together. Put the dough into a buttered bowl and leave it to rise for 1–2 hours, until it has doubled in size.

To make the filling, heat the sugar and butter together in a pan until the sugar has dissolved, then stir in the chocolate and keep it warm enough to stay spreadable. Make the syrup by dissolving the sugar in the water in a pan and simmering it for 2 minutes to thicken. Leave it to cool.

Tip the dough onto a floured work surface then press and roll it out to make a long rectangle about 1cm thick. Spread the filling over the dough leaving a 1cm border around the edge. Scatter over the raspberries and roll up the dough along the long edge, pinching it together around the edges. Lift the dough onto a baking sheet lined with non-stick baking paper. Cut down the centre of the log, leaving one end attached. Carefully plait the two lengths from the joined end along the length, stretching out and twisting the dough to expose the filling. Form the twisted dough into a circle and pinch the join together. Leave to prove, covered in cling film, until doubled in size.

Heat the oven to 180°C/Fan 160°C/Gas 4. Bake the babka for 45–50 minutes, or until it is dark golden brown, risen and cooked through. If the chocolate looks as if it is getting too dark, cover the loaf with a sheet of foil. Brush the babka with the sugar syrup and leave to cool completely.

Per serving 892 kcals, **protein** 14.7g, **carbohydrate** 104.6g, **fat** 44.5g, **saturated fat** 26.6g, **fibre** 5.3g, **salt** 1.3g

Mississippi mud pie

1 hour, plus chilling | serves 8 | a little effort

30 Oreo biscuits (about
  2 packs)
75g butter
500ml double cream, softly
  whipped, to finish

For the cake
50g butter
65g dark chocolate,
  chopped
40ml strong espresso
  coffee
40g ground almonds
3 egg whites (use the yolks
  for the cream, below)
100g golden caster sugar

For the chocolate cream
250ml milk
50g golden caster sugar
3 egg yolks
3 tbsp cornflour
50g dark milk chocolate,
  chopped
100ml double cream

This pie is a chocolate lover's dream. Look for dark milk chocolate for the cream – this is just milk chocolate with a higher cocoa content.

Put the Oreo biscuits (with the filling too) in a food processor and whizz to fine crumbs, then add the butter and whizz again briefly. Press the mixture into the base and up the sides of a 23cm loose-bottomed tart tin (approximately 4cm deep). Freeze while you make the cake mixture.

Heat the oven to 180°C/Fan 160°C/Gas 4. Melt the butter and chocolate with the coffee in a pan, tip it into a bowl and stir in the almonds.

Whisk the egg whites to stiff peaks, then beat in the sugar in three batches and keep whisking until you have a thick glossy meringue. Fold a couple of tablespoons of the meringue into the chocolate mixture, and then fold in the rest. Spoon this mixture into the base, level the top and bake for 30 minutes, or until the cake looks set with a slight wobble in the centre. Cool completely then chill.

Meanwhile, make the chocolate cream, bring the milk to a simmer. Mix the sugar, egg yolks and cornflour to a paste in a bowl and whisk in the milk. Pour the whole lot back into a clean pan and stir it over a low heat until it starts to bubble and thicken. Keep stirring for about 5 minutes over a low heat to make sure the cornflour flavour tastes cooked.

Add the chocolate and cream and stir everything until the chocolate has melted and the custard is smooth. Pour it into a bowl and put a sheet of cling film on the surface of the custard to prevent a skin forming. When the custard is cold, spoon it onto the cake and level the top. Chill the pie until you are ready to eat. Serve with the softly whipped double cream if you like.

Per serving 921 kcals, **protein** 9.1g, **carbohydrate** 55.7g, **fat** 72.8g, **saturated fat** 42g, **fibre** 3.3g, **salt** 0.9g

Carrot cake with maple frosting

2 hours 30 minutes, plus cooling | serves 14 | a little effort

350g carrots, peeled (250g
  halved lengthways)
1 orange, zested and cut
  into 5–6 slices
140g butter, plus extra for
  greasing
140g light soft brown sugar
30g black treacle
70g golden syrup
2 medium eggs, beaten
  with a fork
100ml whole milk
275g plain flour
4 tsp mixed spice
1½ tsp bicarbonate of soda

For the orange frosting

350g unsalted butter, at
  room temperature
375g icing sugar
3 tbsp maple syrup, plus
  extra to serve
3 tbsp orange juice

How do you improve on a classic carrot cake? Roast the carrots for an even denser, richer cake, then slather on maple buttercream.

Heat the oven to 200°C/Fan 180°C/Gas 6. Wrap the halved carrots and orange slices in baking paper to make a parcel, sit it in a roasting tin, then roast for about an hour until really tender.

Put the roasted carrots and two orange slices (not the ends, and discard any remaining slices) in a food processor or blender and whizz to a purée.

Turn the oven down to 160°C/Fan 140°C/Gas 3 and butter and line the base of a deep, round 20cm cake tin. Put the butter, sugar, treacle and syrup in a pan and heat until everything has melted. Leave to cool. Grate the remaining 100g of carrot. Stir in the carrot purée, grated carrot, eggs, orange zest and milk, the flour, mixed spice and bicarb. Scrape the mix into the tin and bake for 1 hour, or until a skewer comes out with crumbs clinging to it. Leave to cool.

For the frosting, put the butter in a big bowl and beat for about 5 minutes until pale and creamy. Sift in the icing sugar then add the maple syrup and orange juice and beat for 3–5 minutes until very fluffy.

Split the cake in three. If you want neatly piped filling, pipe the buttercream in dots using a round nozzle on the bottom 2 layers and chill for 20 minutes to stiffen the icing before sandwiching the cakes together. Otherwise, spread with buttercream then sandwich together. Spread the rest of the frosting on the top, and when ready to serve, drizzle a little maple syrup over the top.

Per serving 535 kcals, **protein** 3.8g, **carbohydrate** 61.7g, **fat** 29.9g, **saturated fat** 18.4g, **fibre** 1.7g, **salt** 0.6g

Easiest-ever chocolate fudge cake

45 minutes | serves 10 | easy

175g butter, softened, plus
  extra for greasing
150g self-raising flour
30g cocoa powder
1 tsp baking powder
175g muscovado sugar
3 eggs
1 tsp vanilla extract
50g dark chocolate, melted

For the fudge icing
200g butter, softened
200g icing sugar
200g dark chocolate,
  melted

No fussing with this cake – just whizz everything together in a food processor then bake!

Heat the oven to 180°C/Fan 160°C/Gas 4. Grease and line two 20cm sandwich tins. Put all the cake ingredients into the food processor and whizz until smooth. If the mix is a little stiff, add a little water and whizz again. Divide between tins, level and bake for 30 minutes or until springy. Leave for 5 minutes then cool on a rack.

Clean the food processor. Whizz the butter and icing sugar until smooth, then add the chocolate and whizz again. Use the icing to sandwich the cake together and spread it on top to finish.

Per serving 646 kcals, **protein** 5.2g, **carbohydrate** 68.3g, **fat** 41g, **saturated fat** 24.4g, **fibre** 1.4g, **salt** 0.97g

Lemon polenta cake

1 hour 45 minutes, plus cooling | serves 10 | easy

350g butter, softened, plus
  extra for greasing
400g caster sugar
4 large eggs
140g polènta
300g ground almonds
1 tsp gluten-free baking
  powder
zest and juice of 4 lemons
2 tbsp flaked almonds,
  toasted (optional)
250g mascarpone
250g crème fraîche
2 tbsp icing sugar
5 tbsp lemon curd

Serve this cake warm with a dollop of mascarpone and it becomes an instant pudding.

Heat the oven to 160°C/Fan 140°C/Gas 3. Butter a round, 23cm springform cake tin and line the base with non-stick baking paper.

Beat the softened butter and 300g of the caster sugar in a big bowl until pale and fluffy, then whisk in the eggs, one at a time. Fold in the polenta, ground almonds and baking powder along with the zest from 3 of the lemons and the juice from 1.

Spoon the mixture into the tin, level the surface and bake for 1–1¼ hours or until a skewer poked into it comes out clean (cover the cake loosely with foil if it browns too much). Meanwhile, make the syrup by heating the remaining 100g of caster sugar in a pan with the juice from the remaining 3 lemons.

When the cake is ready, prick the top all over with a skewer and spoon over the warm syrup. Leave it to cool for 30 minutes in the tin, then remove and leave it to cool completely. Scatter over the flaked almonds, if using, and the remaining zest from 1 lemon.

Beat the mascarpone, crème fraîche, icing sugar and lemon curd together, and chill until ready to serve in a dollop alongside a slice of cooled cake.

Per serving 903 kcals, **protein** 11.8g, **carbohydrate** 53.5g, **fat** 71.7g, **saturated fat** 35.5g, **fibre** 2.7g, **salt** 0.8g

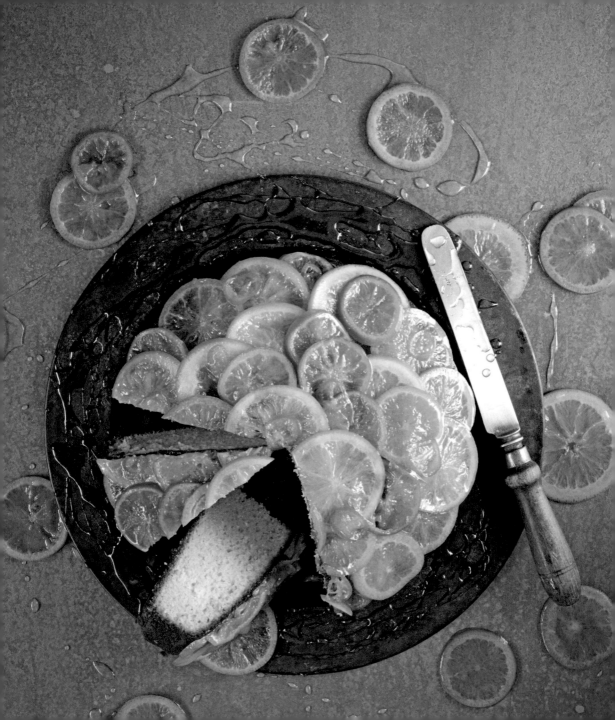

Orange, almond and olive oil cake

1 hour 30 minutes | serves 10 | a little effort

200g plain flour
2 tsp baking powder
pinch of salt
100g ground almonds
275g golden caster sugar
zest of 2 oranges and
  4 tbsp juice
100ml plain yoghurt
4 eggs
1 tsp vanilla extract
160ml extra-virgin olive oil

**For the candied
orange slices**
500g oranges, various sizes
115g golden caster sugar
350ml water

**For the fresh
orange syrup**
200g golden caster sugar
150ml fresh orange juice
75ml water

**This cake is delicious served with Greek yoghurt or whipped cream,
but try not to cover up your beautiful hard work!**

Start with the candied orange slices. Finely slice the oranges into thin
rounds, discarding the two stubby end pieces from each. Dissolve the
caster sugar in the water in a heavy-based pan set over a low heat, stirring
until no sugar crystals remain. Turn the heat up slightly and bring the syrup
to the boil. Add the orange slices and simmer for 15–20 minutes, turning
halfway, until the orange slices are tender but still hold their shape. Cool,
then transfer to a wire rack and leave to cool in a single layer. Discard the
cooking liquid.

To make the fresh orange syrup, put the sugar in a saucepan with the
orange juice and the water. Slowly bring to the boil, simmer for 5 minutes
until thickened slightly, then leave to cool.

Heat the oven to 180°C/Fan 160°C/Gas 4 and line the base and sides of
a 23cm springform tin with non-stick baking paper. Sift the flour, baking
powder and a pinch of salt into a bowl then mix in the almonds. In a
separate bowl, whisk the sugar, orange zest and juice, yoghurt, eggs and
vanilla extract. Gradually whisk in the dry ingredients to form a smooth
batter. Fold in the oil to finish. Pour the mixture into the tin and bake for
45–50 minutes, until golden and risen and a skewer pushed into the centre
comes out clean. Pierce the cake all over with a skewer and douse with
6 tablespoons of orange syrup, reserving the rest.

Arrange the orange slices on the top of the cake and, just before serving,
pour the remaining syrup over the top.

Per serving 573 kcals, **protein** 7.8g, **carbohydrate** 79.5g, **fat** 24.4g, **saturated fat** 3.6g, **fibre** 2g, **salt** 0.4g

White chocolate and raspberry cheesecake

1 hour, plus chilling | serves 10 | easy

300g white chocolate
  chunk cookies
50g butter, melted
600g cream cheese
2 tbsp plain flour
175g golden caster sugar
a few drops of vanilla
  extract
2 eggs, plus 1 yolk
150ml pot of soured cream
300g raspberries, fresh or
  frozen
100g white chocolate,
  chopped into small
  pieces
1 tbsp icing sugar
2–3 tbsp framboise
  (optional)

Raspberry cheesecake is the most popular recipe on our website. It's updated here, with added chocolate and booze. The framboise bumps up the raspberry flavour and makes this a more grown-up dessert.

Heat the oven to 180°C/Fan 160°C/Gas 4. Crush the cookies in a food processor or put them in a plastic bag and bash with a rolling pin. Tip the crumbs into a bowl with the melted butter and stir to coat them. Press the mixture into a 20cm diameter springform tin and bake for 5 minutes. Leave to cool.

Beat the cream cheese with the flour, sugar, vanilla, eggs, the yolk and soured cream until light and fluffy. Stir in half the raspberries and all the white chocolate pieces and spoon into the tin. Bake for 40 minutes and then check – it should be set but slightly wobbly in the centre. Leave in the tin to cool completely, then chill for 2 hours.

Just before serving, put most of the remaining raspberries in a pan with 1 tablespoon of icing sugar (keep a few raspberries aside). Heat until juicy and then squash with a fork. Push them through a sieve, then mix the purée with the framboise (if using) and the whole raspberries and serve with the cheesecake.

Per serving 648 kcals, **protein** 8.8g, **carbohydrate** 42.2g, **fat** 50g, **saturated fat** 29.4g, **fibre** 0.8g, **salt** 0.7g

Passion fruit layer cake

45 minutes, plus cooling | serves 8–10 | easy

200g butter, softened, plus
extra for greasing
200g golden caster sugar
4 eggs
200g self-raising flour,
sifted
a splash of milk

For the passion fruit icing

4 passion fruit
100g butter, softened
200g icing sugar, plus extra
for dusting

An easy-to-make, springy sponge cake layered with the tangy, fresh-tasting sweetness of passion fruit icing.

Heat the oven to 180°C/Fan 160°C/Gas 4. Grease and line two 20cm sponge tins. Beat the sugar and butter together until the mixture is soft, then beat in the eggs, flour and milk to make a smooth batter that will drop easily off a spoon. Divide the mixture between the tins and smooth the top of the batter. Bake the cakes for 20–25 minutes, or until the sponges are risen, golden and springy. Leave to cool.

Halve the passion fruit and scoop the seeds and pulp into a sieve set over a bowl. Stir the pulp until all the juices have been pushed through. Beat the butter until it is very light, then beat in most of the icing sugar until the mixture thickens. Beat in 2 tablespoons of passion fruit juice followed by the remaining icing sugar.

Brush the two inside faces of the sponges with the remaining passion fruit juice. Lay one half juice-side up on plate, spread on the icing and then gently press the top layer on, juice-side down. Dust the top with icing sugar.

Per serving 486 kcals, **protein** 4.8g, **carbohydrate** 54.9g, **fat** 27.2g, **saturated fat** 16.3g, **fibre** 1.1g, **salt** 0.7g

Chocolate and almond cake

45 minutes | serves 12 | easy

200g unsalted butter, plus
   extra for greasing
flour, for dusting
200g dark chocolate (75%
   cocoa solids or above)
250g caster sugar
5 eggs, separated
250g blanched almonds,
   finely chopped in a food
   processor
finely grated zest of
   1 unwaxed lemon
cocoa powder or icing
   sugar, for dusting

To serve
250g mascarpone
1 tsp vanilla extract
1 tbsp icing sugar
150g raspberries

If you're in the mood for a light chocolate cake that is easy to make, this is perfect for you.

Heat the oven to 190°C/Fan 170°C/Gas 5. Grease and flour a 23cm loose-bottomed round cake tin.

Break the chocolate into a large heatproof bowl set over a saucepan of simmering water, making sure the base doesn't touch the water, and heat until the chocolate has melted. Add the butter in pieces and mix until smooth. Mix in the sugar followed by the egg yolks. Remove from the heat and add the almonds.

Whisk the egg whites in a bowl until they form peaks. Add the lemon zest, then fold gently into the chocolate mixture until blended. Pour the mixture into the prepared tin and bake for 30–45 minutes, or until the cake is golden brown and has pulled away from the sides of the tin. Turn the cake out onto a wire rack, leave to cool and then dust with cocoa or icing sugar.

Mix the mascarpone and vanilla extract together with the icing sugar. Serve with the cake and some raspberries.

Per serving 561 kcals, **protein** 9.9g, **carbohydrate** 30.1g, **fat** 43.9g, **saturated fat** 20.4g, **fibre** 2.3g, **salt** 0.1g

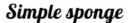

Simple sponge

40 minutes, plus cooling | serves 8 | easy

175g unsalted butter, at
room temperature
175g golden caster sugar
175g self-raising flour,
sifted
1 tsp baking powder
1 tsp vanilla extract
3 eggs
1–2 tbsp milk (optional)

For the filling
4 tbsp strawberry jam
142ml double cream,
whipped
icing sugar, for dusting

A classic, simple Victoria sponge is one of the recipes that you should have in your repertoire. Once you master this, bake sales and afternoon tea will no longer be daunting, and making variations will be easy.

Heat the oven to 180°C/Fan 160°C/Gas 4. Line and butter two 18cm sandwich tins with non-stick baking paper. Beat all the cake ingredients together in a large bowl, adding the milk if the mixture is too stiff to drop off a spoon when tapped gently. Divide the mixture between the tins and level the surfaces.

Bake side by side for 20–25 minutes until the sponges are risen, slightly shrunk away from the edge of the tin and spring back when lightly pressed. Leave to cool for 5 minutes then turn out onto a rack and peel off the paper. Cool completely before filling.

Spread the jam onto the base of one sponge. Spread the cream on top of the jam. Sandwich the other sponge on top. Dust with icing sugar.

Per slice 470 kcals, **protein** 5.2g, **carbohydrate** 47.2g, **fat** 30.3g, **saturated fat** 17.4g, **fibre** 0.7g, **salt** 0.49g

Texas sheet cake

1 hour, plus cooling | serves 20 | easy

200g butter
200g golden caster sugar
200g light muscovado
  sugar
250ml water
250g self-raising flour
5 tbsp cocoa powder
a pinch of baking powder
2 eggs
125g soured cream
2 handfuls of mini
  marshmallows (optional)

For the frosting
175g butter
3 tbsp cocoa powder
2 tbsp soured cream
100g milk chocolate,
  chopped
200g icing sugar

This cake is a southern American specialty. Made with soured cream and cocoa, it is so moist everyone will ask for the recipe.

Heat the oven to 180°C/Fan 160°C/Gas 4. To make the cake, put the butter, sugars and the water in a pan and heat gently until the butter has melted. Take the pan off the heat and stir in the flour, cocoa, baking powder, eggs and soured cream to a smooth batter, then stir in the marshmallows, if using. Pour the mixture into a lined 20 x 30cm baking tray (leave some paper overhanging to help you lift it out) and cook for 25–30 minutes. Cool, then lift out.

For the frosting, melt the butter and 2 tablespoons of the cocoa together and add the soured cream and chopped chocolate. Add the icing sugar and stir until smooth, then cool completely. Don't worry if the butter separates; it'll come back when you beat it. Once cold, beat with electric beaters until the frosting is paler and fluffier. Spread the frosting over the cake and dust with the remaining tablespoon of cocoa.

Per serving 368 kcals, **protein** 3.6g, **carbohydrate** 42g, **fat** 20.6g, **saturated fat** 12.6g, **fibre** 1.6g, **salt** 0.6g

Strawberry and pistachio cake

1 hour 15 minutes | serves 12 | a little effort

200g pistachios
275g golden caster sugar
250g butter
3 eggs
275g self-raising flour
75g full-fat Greek yoghurt
splash of milk (optional)

For the strawberry icing
200g butter
300g icing sugar
300g small ripe
   strawberries, hulled

A lovely summer pistachio cake with strawberry icing that's worth the extra effort. When strawberries smell good, they should be at optimum ripeness and have flavour – perfect for this cake.

Heat the oven to 180°C/Fan 160°C/Gas 4 and line a square cake tin about 20 x 20cm with non-stick baking paper. Put 150g of the pistachios into a food processor with half the sugar, then whizz until very finely chopped. Tip them into a large mixing bowl, add the remaining sugar and beat in the butter until it is creamy. Beat in the eggs, flour and yoghurt until smooth. Add a splash of milk if the mixture needs it.

Spoon the mixture into the tin, level the top and bake for 45–50 minutes or until a skewer inserted into the middle comes out clean. Cool for 15 minutes and then turn out onto a serving platter or board and peel off the paper. Leave to cool.

To make the icing, beat the butter until white and fluffy, then beat in the sugar a little at a time. When the mix feels stiff, add 4 strawberries and beat them in until they are mashed into a pulp. Beat in the remaining sugar. If the mix is still stiff, beat in another strawberry.

Cover the top and sides of the cake with the icing. Whizz the remaining pistachios until finely chopped and press against the edge of the cake. Just before serving, thinly slice the remaining strawberries and lay them neatly in rows on the top of the cake, with each row running the opposite way from the one next to it.

Per serving 671 kcals, **protein** 7.8g, **carbohydrate** 67.6g, **fat** 40.7g, **saturated fat** 21.3g, **fibre** 3g, **salt** 0.9g

Plum and almond sheet cake

1 hour, plus cooling | serves 12 | easy

200g butter, plus extra for greasing
200g light muscovado sugar
4 eggs
150g self-raising flour
50g ground almonds
250g soft cheese
400g plums, halved and pitted
about 15 Marcona almonds
1 tsp ground cinnamon
1 tsp vanilla paste

This open fruit tart looks and tastes fantastic with very little effort. Accompany with a dollop of whipped double cream or crème fraîche.

Heat the oven to 180°C/Fan 160°C/Gas 4. Beat 175g of the butter until smooth, then beat in 175g of the sugar, 3 of the eggs, the flour and the ground almonds. The mixture should be quite thick. Spoon it into a greased and lined rectangular tin about 18 x 28cm.

Beat the soft cheese with the remaining egg plus 1 tablespoon of the remaining sugar. Spoon this in clumps onto the top of the cake mix.

Press the plums, skin-side down in rows into the cake mix. Put a Marcona almond into the middle of each plum. Melt the remaining butter with the last bit of sugar, the cinnamon and the vanilla paste and brush this over the plums and almonds, drizzle any remainder over the cake mix. Bake for 40–45 minutes or until the cake is golden and puffed around the plums.

Per serving 376 kcals, **protein** 6.5g, **carbohydrate** 28.7g, **fat** 26g, **saturated fat** 13.8g, **fibre** 1.2g, **salt** 0.6g

Show-off cakes

Strawberry eclairs

2 hours, plus cooling | makes 10–12 | a little effort

150g plain flour

1 tbsp caster sugar

75g unsalted butter, cut into 1cm cubes, plus extra for greasing

75ml milk, plus a splash extra

125ml water

4 eggs (3 lightly beaten and 1 yolk)

400ml double cream, whipped with 2 tbsp icing sugar

5 strawberries, hulled and sliced

freeze-dried strawberries, crushed, to decorate (optional)

For the strawberry glaze

2 big or 4 small strawberries

200g icing sugar

These eclairs take some time to make but are perfect for the British strawberry season. Serve as a surprise treat for friends and family.

Heat the oven to 180°C/Fan 160°C/Gas 4 and line a baking sheet with non-stick baking paper. Sift the flour into a bowl. Put the sugar, butter and milk in a pan with the water and bring to the boil. Take the pan off the heat, pour in the flour and beat the mixture until it turns into a smooth, thick pastry dough that comes away from the side of the pan. Tip it into the bowl of a stand mixer and beat it for a couple of minutes to cool it down.

Add the whole eggs gradually (the mixture should be thick enough to hold its shape so you may not need all the egg), beating all the time. Don't worry if the mixture looks as if it has split – it will come back. Scrape the mix into a piping bag fitted with a plain round nozzle about 1½cm wide and pipe eclairs about 12cm long onto the baking sheet, spacing them well apart. Beat the yolk with a splash of milk and paint a wide stripe of egg wash down the top of each eclair. Bake for 50 minutes or until the eclairs are completely dry – check by cutting one in half horizontally. If they are still soggy they will collapse when they cool. Cool completely.

To make the glaze, squash the strawberries and add a couple of tablespoons of icing sugar and mash everything together well, leaving it for 5 minutes. Push the lot through a fine sieve and use this as a base – you can add more icing sugar to it, or as much water as you need, to make a thick icing that will stay on the top of the eclairs without running off.

Halve the eclairs horizontally. Dip the lids, top-down, in the icing and put them cut-side down to dry. If your icing is thin, dip the lids until they look thicker. Spoon the whipped cream into a piping bag fitted with a wide nozzle and then pipe a strip of cream along each base. Arrange a layer of overlapping strawberry slices on top and then pipe on a couple of small dots of cream to help the lid stay on. Repeat with all the eclairs and then put a lid on each. Sprinkle with dried strawberries, if you like.

Per serving 445 kcals, **protein** 4.7g, **carbohydrate** 37.5g, **fat** 30.5g, **saturated fat** 18.2g, **fibre** 0.7g, **salt** 0.1g

Strawberry dream

1½ hours, plus chilling | serves 10 | a little effort

6 eggs

175g golden caster sugar, plus extra for dusting

175g self-raising flour

50g butter, melted

1 tsp vanilla extract

For the filling

400g strawberries

2 tbsp golden caster sugar

zest of 1 orange

300g mascarpone

100g condensed milk

For the frosting

200g white granulated sugar

4 tbsp water

2 large egg whites

½ tsp vanilla extract

Truly living up to its name, you will want to keep this cake all to yourself. Perfect to make at the height of the British strawberry season.

Heat the oven to 200°C/Fan 180°C/Gas 6. Line a 27 x 37cm Swiss roll tin with non-stick baking paper. Whisk the eggs and sugar together until they are really light and fluffy – this can take about 5 minutes. Fold in the flour, then gradually fold in the butter and vanilla. Spoon the mix into the tin, level and bake for 12–15 minutes until pale but springy and cooked in the middle. Leave to cool.

To make the filling, finely chop 300g of the largest strawberries and place them in a sieve set over a bowl, then sprinkle over the caster sugar. Leave for 1 hour for the strawberries to release their juice. Keep the juice, and squash the strawberries lightly against the sieve to extract as much juce as possible.

Stir the orange zest, mascarpone, condensed milk and strawberry pulp together. Line a 900g loaf tin with non-stick baking paper. Lay the loaf tin on the sponge and cut a strip just wide enough to fit in the tin – the length should fit as the sponge will have shrunk, but trim it if not. Put this in the base of the tin and brush the top with the strawberry juice. Add half the filling. Cut another strip of sponge a little wider than the last and add this, brush on the remaining juice and add the remaining filling. Add the last piece of sponge and freeze the cake for an hour.

To make the frosting, put the sugar and water in a pan. Slowly increase the heat and boil until you have a thick, clear syrup. Meanwhile, in a separate bowl beat the egg whites until stiff, then pour in the hot sugar syrup in a steady stream, beating until the mixture is fluffy and thick and the frosting is cool. Stir in the vanilla. Turn the cake out carefully onto a plate and remove the paper, cover it with the frosting and decorate with the remaining strawberries.

Per serving 494 kcals, **protein**, 8.7g, **carbohydrate** 62.4g, **fat** 22.8g, **saturated fat** 14.1g, **fibre** 1.3g, **salt** 0.4g

Pistachio and chocolate roulade

50 minutes, plus cooling | serves 12 | a little effort

135g self-raising flour
40g good-quality cocoa
    powder
6 eggs
175g golden caster sugar,
    plus extra for dusting
50g butter, melted
300ml double cream,
    whipped
100g 72% dark chocolate,
    chopped
slivered pistachios, to
    decorate

For the pistachio filling
150g white chocolate,
    finely chopped
100g pistachio paste
    (or same weight of finely
    ground peeled
    pistachios)
100ml double cream

The most beautiful slivered green pistachios to top this cake can be found online and in some Middle-Eastern shops, but you can use crushed green pistachios if you can't find them.

Heat the oven to 200°C/Fan 180°C/Gas 6. Line a 29 x 40cm Swiss roll tin or similar with non-stick baking paper. Sift the flour and cocoa together. Whisk the eggs and sugar together until they are light and fluffy, this can take about 5 minutes, so keep going until they are really fluffy. Fold in the flour and cocoa then carefully fold in the butter. Spoon the mix into the tin, level the surface and bake for 15–20 minutes until cooked and springy in the middle.

Leave to cool a little then turn the sponge out onto another sheet of baking paper dusted with sugar. Roll it up like a Swiss roll, keeping the paper sandwiched between the cake layers, and cool completely.

To make the filling, put the chocolate and pistachio paste in a bowl, heat the cream to boiling, pour this over and stir until smooth. Leave to cool completely and thicken in the fridge.

When the sponge is completely cool, unroll it carefully and spread it with the pistachio filling followed by the whipped cream, then roll it up like a Swiss roll again, this time without the paper in between. Put it on a plate or board, seam-side down. Melt the dark chocolate and pour it backwards and forwards over the roll. Sprinkle over the slivered pistachios.

Per serving 504 kcals, **protein** 8.6g, **carbohydrate** 34.6g, **fat** 36.2g, **saturated fat** 19.3g, **fibre** 2.8g, **salt** 0.4g

Lemon and white chocolate layer loaf

45 minutes, plus chilling | serves 6-8 | a little effort

175g butter, plus extra for
  greasing
175g golden caster sugar,
  plus 1 tbsp
3 eggs
150g self-raising flour
½ tsp baking powder
50g ground almonds
zest and juice of 2 lemons

For the icing
200g white chocolate
25g butter
zest and juice of 1 lemon

The sweetness of the white chocolate offsets the lemon tart for a perfectly balanced loaf.

Heat the oven to 180°C/Fan 160°C/Gas 4. Grease and line a brownie tin approximately 27 x 18cm. Beat the butter and 175g of the sugar together until creamy then add the eggs, flour and baking powder, and finally the ground almonds. Beat again before folding in the lemon zest and half of the juice.

Scoop the mixture into the tin and level the top – you need the cake to be flat when it's baked. Bake for 20–25 minutes or until cooked and very lightly browned. Cool the cake in the tin and then on a wire rack. Mix the remaining lemon juice and 1 tablespoon of caster sugar together and brush this over the top of the cooled cake.

For the icing, melt the chocolate, butter and half of the lemon zest and all the juice together in a heatproof bowl set over a pan of simmering water (don't let the bowl touch the water). You could also do this in short bursts in the microwave. Stir until smooth and then cool until thick enough to spread.

Cut the cake into three equal strips and trim the tops if you need to. Spread some icing on one layer, put another strip on top, ice again and then finish with the final strip, but don't ice it yet. Chill the cake for an hour so that it can firm up then trim any brown edges and ice the top (warm the icing in the microwave if you need to soften it). Sprinkle on the remaining zest and leave the cake to set before slicing.

Per serving 544 kcals, **protein** 7.5g, **carbohydrate** 52.5g, **fat** 34.1g, **saturated fat** 18.5g, **fibre** 0.8g, **salt** 0.8g

Rhubarb Bakewell tart

1½ hours | serves 6 | easy

500g sweet shortcrust
   pastry
50g plain flour, plus extra
   for dusting
300g rhubarb, trimmed but
   stalks left whole
175g golden caster sugar
2 tbsp strawberry jam
125g butter, softened
2 medium eggs
125g ground almonds
½ tsp baking powder
1 heaped tbsp flaked
   almonds
icing sugar, to decorate
   (optional)
clotted cream, to serve

This is a modern twist on a British favourite made using rhubarb. It's easy to make but looks impressive. Be sure to use rhubarb when it is in season from February until May.

Roll out the pastry on a lightly dusted work surface and use it to line a 23cm round tart tin. Leave the excess pastry hanging over the tin, prick the base with a fork and chill for 30 minutes.

Meanwhile, heat the oven to 180°C/Fan 160°C/Gas 4. Lay the rhubarb stalks in a snug baking dish, scatter over 50g of the sugar and cover tightly with foil. Bake for 20–30 minutes, or until the rhubarb is tender, but not mushy, when poked with a knife. Leave to cool.

Increase the oven temperature to 190°C/Fan 170°C/Gas 5. Line the pastry case with some crumpled greaseproof paper, fill with baking beans and bake for 15 minutes. Remove the beans and paper and bake for another 5 minutes, then leave to cool.

Trim the rhubarb to fit across the tart with enough room in between each stalk to let some sponge show through. Spread the jam over the base of the cooled tart case.

Beat the butter with the remaining caster sugar, the eggs, ground almonds, flour and baking powder. Dollop this into the tart, gently spreading it out evenly. Arrange the rhubarb on top, scatter over the flaked almonds and bake for 25–30 minutes, or until the sponge is risen and golden.

Eat warm or at room temperature (dust with icing sugar, if you like), with a generous spoon of clotted cream alongside each wedge.

Per serving 877 kcals, **protein** 14.7g, **carbohydrate** 77.9g, **fat** 17.1g, **saturated fat** 19.7g, **fibre** 3.4g, **salt** 1.3g

Upside-down apple and star anise cake

1 hour 20 minutes | serves 6 | easy

100g butter, plus extra for
  greasing
100g dark muscovado
  sugar
100g self-raising flour
1 tsp baking powder
a large pinch of ground
  ginger
a large pinch of ground
  cinnamon
2 eggs
pinch of salt
double cream, whipped,
  or ice cream, to serve

For the topping
50g butter
50g golden caster sugar
2–3 whole star anise
3–5 apples, peeled, cored
  and cut into thin slices

Turning a cake into something even more special is easy when you make it upside-down. Sticky apple slices and a hint of star anise in this recipe makes an easy dinner-party dessert or the best family pud.

Heat the oven to 180°C/Fan 160°C/Gas 4. Make the topping by melting the butter and caster sugar together in a pan with the star anise until the sugar has dissolved. Leave to cool a little.

Pour the melted mixture into a buttered 20cm springform cake tin. Put the star anise on opposite sides of the tin, then use the apple slices to line the base of the tin, placing them in concentric circles.

Beat the butter and muscovado sugar together until the mixture is pale and creamy, then beat in the flour, baking powder, ginger, cinnamon and eggs, along with a pinch of salt. Spoon this onto the apples and level the top. Bake for 30–35 minutes or until the sponge is cooked through. Leave to cool for 5 minutes, then turn out the cake carefully onto a plate. Serve with cream or ice cream.

per serving 406 kcal, **protein** 4.2g, **carbohydrates** 44.9g, **fat** 22.7g, **saturated fat** 13.6g, **fibre** 2.3g, **salt** 0.9g

Chocolate tiramisu torte

1 hour | serves 12 | a little effort

300g unsalted butter, at
  room temperature, plus
  extra for greasing
270g self-raising flour
1½ tsp baking powder
300g golden caster sugar
6 eggs
4 tbsp cocoa
2 tbsp instant coffee,
  dissolved in 1 tbsp
  boiling water

For the filling
100ml espresso or strong
  instant coffee, cooled
4 tbsp Tia Maria
250ml tub of mascarpone
568ml pot of double
  cream
1 tbsp Amaretto
50g dark chocolate, finely
  grated

This devilish combination of Amaretto, Tia Maria, mascarpone and dark chocolate comes together to make our best ever tiramisu torte – it's well worth the effort.

Heat the oven to 180°C/Fan 160°C/Gas 4. Grease and line the base of two 20cm cake tins with non-stick baking paper. Put all the cake ingredients in a food processor and blend until smooth. Divide the mixture between the tins and cook for 25–30 minutes or until the sponge is springy. Cool completely then cut each cake in half horizontally.

To make the filling, mix the coffee with 2 tablespoons of the Tia Maria and sprinkle over the cut sides of each cake. Beat the mascarpone until it softens then stir in the cream, bit by bit. Add the remaining Tia Maria and the Amaretto then whisk until softly whipped.

Sandwich the 4 layers together with the boozy cream in between each, leaving plenty for the top. Finish the top with a layer of cream and finely grated dark chocolate. Chill for an hour before serving to make the cake easier to cut.

Per serving 784 kcals, **protein** 7.6g, **carbohydrate** 50.7g, **fat** 61.1g, **saturated fat** 35.2g, **fibre** 1g, **salt** 0.6g

Fluffy coconut and lime cake

1 hour, plus cooling | serves 10 | a little effort

200g caster sugar
200g butter, softened
4 eggs, beaten
200g self-raising flour
1 tsp baking powder
zest and juice of 1 lime
½ x 200g block creamed
   coconut, grated
sweetened coconut flakes,
   to decorate

For the frosting
2 egg whites
200g granulated sugar
4 tbsp water
½ tsp vanilla extract

This indulgent coconut and lime cake hits all the afternoon tea spots. Topped with vanilla frosting and coconut flakes, this is the perfect weekend baking project. Look for big coconut flakes rather than dessicated coconut to get a dramatic finish.

Heat the oven to 190°C/Fan 170°C/Gas 5. Line two 20cm sandwich tins with non-stick baking paper. Beat the sugar, butter, eggs, flour, baking powder, lime zest and juice and creamed coconut together. Divide the mixture between the cake tins, level off the surface and bake for 20 minutes or until risen and golden. Cool completely.

To make the frosting, whisk the egg whites to stiff peaks. Combine the sugar with the water and boil until you have a thick, clear syrup. Beat the syrup into the egg whites, adding it in a thin stream, and stir in the vanilla.

Sandwich the cakes together with frosting then frost the top and sides. Gently press flakes of coconut all over the sides.

Per serving 488 kcals, **protein** 5.8g, **carbohydrate** 59.6g, **fat** 26.9g, **saturated fat** 17.9g, **fibre** 0.9g, **salt** 0.77g

Roman cheesecake

1½ hours | serves 8 | a little effort

2 tbsp seedless raisins
3 tbsp Marsala or Amaretto
unsalted butter, for
    greasing
2 tbsp fresh white
    breadcrumbs
675g ricotta
115g runny honey
3 eggs, separated
finely grated zest of
    1 lemon

For the decoration

2 ripe peaches, sliced, or
    use peach compote or
    peaches in liqueur
3 tbsp apricot jam (if using
    fresh peaches)

Topped with peaches and with a ricotta and honey base, this is light, yet rich and creamy.

Soak the raisins in the liqueur for 30 minutes. Heat the oven to 160°C/Fan 140°C/Gas 3. Generously grease the base and sides of an 18cm springform or loose-bottomed cake tin. Dust with the breadcrumbs, covering both the base and sides as evenly as possible.

Sift the ricotta into a large bowl and beat in the honey and egg yolks. Stir in the soaked raisins with the lemon zest. Whisk the egg whites in a separate bowl until they are firm but not dry, then fold them into the cheese mixture.

Pour the mixture into the tin and bake for 40–50 minutes, or until a skewer inserted in the centre comes out clean. Leave in the tin to cool completely.

Remove the tin and transfer the cheesecake to a plate. To decorate, arrange the peaches over the top. Heat the jam gently with a splash of water in a small pan, then spoon over the peaches to glaze.

Per serving 252 kcals, **protein** 11g, **carbohydrate** 21.8g, **fat** 12g, **saturated fat** 6.7g, **fibre** 0.6g, **salt** 0.4g

White chocolate fudge cake

1 hour, plus cooling | serves 12 | easy

300g butter, softened, plus
  extra for greasing
150g white chocolate,
  chopped, plus extra,
  grated, to serve
5 eggs
150g golden caster sugar
150g light soft brown sugar
½ tsp vanilla extract
300g self-raising flour
½ tsp baking powder

For the frosting
5 tbsp plain flour
250ml whole milk
150g white chocolate,
  chopped
1 tsp vanilla extract
225g butter, softened
200g golden caster sugar

This white chocolate cake has an American-style whipped frosting, which is lighter than a ganache or buttercream.

Heat the oven to 180°C/Fan 160°C/Gas 4. Grease and line three 20cm sponge tins with non-stick baking paper. Melt the butter and chocolate carefully together, then pour the melted mixture into the bowl of a mixer and cool for 10 minutes. Don't worry if it separates when it cools.

Beat the butter and chocolate mixture for a couple of minutes and then beat in the eggs one by one, alternating them with batches of both sugars. Add the vanilla, the flour and baking powder and beat on low to make a smooth batter. Divide the mixture between the sponge tins and bake for 20–25 minutes or until the edges come away from the sides of the tin and a skewer comes out clean. Be careful not to overcook the cake or it will go very brown as there is a lot of sugar in it. Cool in the tin for 10 minutes, then transfer it to a wire rack.

To make the frosting, whisk the flour into the milk in a pan over a medium heat, whisking until the mixture thickens. Stir in the chocolate and vanilla and leave to cool. Beat the butter and sugar together until they're light and fluffy, then beat in the chocolate mix until you have a light, fluffy mixture. Layer the cakes up with some of the frosting and then frost the outside. Decorate by grating over some more white chocolate.

Per serving 784 kcals, **protein** 8.9g, **carbohydrate** 80.8g, **fat** 46.8g, **saturated fat** 28.3g, **fibre** 1.4g, **salt** 1.1g

Devil's food cake with orange frosting

2 hours 30 minutes | serves 10 | easy

125ml rapeseed or
   grapeseed oil, plus extra
   for greasing
100g light muscovado
   sugar
150g golden caster sugar
50g cocoa powder
225g self-raising flour
½ tsp baking powder
2 eggs
2 oranges, zest of 2,
   juice of 1
50g dark chocolate, melted
   and cooled

For the icing
250g butter, softened
500g icing sugar
2 oranges, zest of 2,
   juice of 1

This version of devil's food cake is made with oil rather than butter, and has orange added to the flavour. It's a cake that cuts neatly and works well as a base for all sorts of icing.

Heat the oven to 160°C/Fan 140°C/Gas 3. Oil and line two 20cm cake tins with tight-fitting bases with non-stick baking paper. Put the sugars in the bowl of a mixer and sift over the cocoa, flour and baking powder. Mix the eggs with the oil and orange zest in a jug and add them to the bowl, beating a couple of times. Put the orange juice in the jug and add enough water to make 250ml, then add this to the bowl.

Beat the ingredients slowly to mix everything together then add the melted chocolate. Beat for 3 minutes until the mixture is smooth – it should be runnier than a normal cake mix. Scoop the mixture into the cake tins, dividing it as equally as you can, and level the tops. Bake for 30 minutes or until the cakes are cooked through – test them with a skewer, it should come out clean. Cool for 10 minutes in the tins then turn the cakes out onto a wire rack.

To make the frosting, beat the butter until it is really soft, then beat in the icing sugar a little at a time. Add the orange zest and a splash of juice and beat until the frosting is fluffy. Sandwich the cakes together with some frosting then frost the outside of the cake.

Per serving 733 kcals, **protein** 4.8g, **carbohydrate** 94.6g, **fat** 37.7g, **saturated fat** 16.1g, **fibre** 2.4g, **salt** 0.8g

Vanilla, chocolate and caramel layer cake

1 hour, plus cooling and chilling | serves 12 | tricky but worth it

225g unsalted butter, very
  soft, plus extra for
  greasing
350g white caster sugar
4 large eggs
2 tsp vanilla extract
350g self-raising flour
pinch of salt
120ml soured cream, at
  room temperature

For the caramel filling
225g white caster sugar
100ml water
250ml double cream
40g unsalted butter
1 tsp vanilla extract or
  vanilla bean paste
pinch of salt

**For the chocolate
frosting**
250g dark chocolate,
  chopped
175g unsalted butter,
  softened
100g golden icing sugar
2 tbsp golden syrup
1 tsp vanilla extract
chocolate sprinkles, to
  decorate

Soured cream gives a lovely soft texture to this cake. Using white sugar to make caramel makes it much easier to see what the colour is, especially if you are using a dark pan, or you could use a tin or jar of ready-made caramel if you want a shortcut.

To make the caramel filling, tip the sugar into a pan with the water. Heat until the sugar dissolves then bring the syrup to the boil and continue to cook until it becomes a rich golden caramel. Take the pan off the heat and very carefully add the remaining ingredients – it will hiss and splutter, so be careful. Return the pan to a gentle heat for a minute or so to re-melt any hardened caramel and stir until smooth. Scoop the caramel into a bowl and leave until completely cold and thickened to a spreadable consistency. You can put the caramel into the fridge to speed up the thickening process.

Grease and line the base of three 20cm sandwich tins with discs of greased baking paper. Heat the oven to 180°C/Fan 160°C/Gas 4.

Cream the butter and caster sugar together with electric beaters until really pale and light. Lightly beat the eggs and vanilla extract. Gradually add the eggs to the creamed butter and sugar in 4–5 batches, mixing well and scraping down the bowl in between each.

Sift the flour and a pinch of salt into the bowl, add the soured cream and mix until smooth. Divide the mix evenly between the tins and level the tops. Bake for 20–25 minutes until risen and golden and a wooden skewer inserted into the middle of the cakes comes out clean. Cool the cakes in the tins for 4 minutes then turn out to cool.

To make the chocolate frosting, melt the chocolate in a heatproof bowl over a pan of barely simmering water, making sure the base doesn't touch the water. Stir until smooth and remove from the heat to cool slightly. Cream the butter and icing sugar until smooth, pale and light. Add the golden syrup and vanilla and mix. Add the melted chocolate and beat until smooth and glossy.

To assemble the cake, slice each of the cake layers in half so that you have six even layers. Put the bottom layer of one cake on a serving plate and spread with one-third of the caramel filling. Top with a second cake layer. Spread this with 2 tablespoons of chocolate filling. Repeat this layering, alternating the fillings until you have six layers of cake filled with three layers of caramel and two of chocolate. Cover the top of and sides of the cake with the remaining chocolate mixture, then scatter with chocolate sprinkles.

Per serving 848 kcals, **protein** 6.7g **carbohydrate** 90.7g, **fat** 51g, **saturated fat** 31.1g, **fibre** 1.9g, **salt** 0.5g

Grapefruit and poppy seed angel cake

1 hour 40 minutes, plus cooling | serves 8-10 | a little effort

---

150g plain flour

225g white caster sugar

1 tbsp cornflour

2 tbsp poppy seeds

12 large egg whites (or use
a carton of whites)

1 tsp cream of tartar

½ tsp fine sea salt

zest of 1 red grapefruit and
1 tbsp juice

zest of 1 pink grapefruit

70g icing sugar, sifted

For the sugared peel

1 red grapefruit

100g white caster sugar,
plus extra for sprinkling
over peel

For the icing

200g white chocolate,
finely chopped

100ml double cream

100g icing sugar, sifted

You'll need an angel cake tin for this as the cake won't rise properly in a conventional tin. You can buy these from good cookshops online.

Heat the oven to 180°C/Fan 160°C/Gas 4. Sift the flour with the caster sugar and cornflour, stir through the poppy seeds and put to one side.

Whisk the egg whites with the cream of tartar, salt, grapefruit zest and juice until foamy using an electric whisk. Gradually add the icing sugar a spoonful at a time, whisking until firm peaks form. Add the flour mixture in 2 batches, using a large metal spoon to fold it in gently to retain the air, making sure there are no pockets of flour. Put the mixture into a clean, dry 25 x 10cm angel cake tin and level out with the back of a spoon (it's important not to butter the tin). Bake for 45–50 minutes or until a skewer comes out clean and the cake springs back when lightly pressed. Remove from the oven, turn the tin upside down and leave to cool in the tin for 1 hour.

Meanwhile, make the sugared peel by peeling the remaining grapefruit with a swivel peeler, leaving the white pith behind. Cut the strips into fine matchsticks, boil in water for 5 minutes and drain. Put the peel back into the empty pan. Juice the grapefruit and add 150ml of the juice to the saucepan with the sugar. Dissolve the sugar over a gentle heat before boiling the peel for 5-7 minutes until the peel is candied. Remove the peel with a slotted spoon, separate out on some baking paper and cool. Toss the peel with the sugar to coat and leave to dry.

To remove the cake, run a palette knife around the inner and outer edges of the tin until the cake comes away. Remove it from the tin and put it bottom-side up on a cake stand.

For the icing, melt the white chocolate, cream and icing sugar in a saucepan over a low heat, stirring until just melted. Spoon on top of the cake while still warm, working quickly as it will start to set. Top with the sugared peel to serve.

Per serving 422 kcals, **protein** 7g **carbohydrate** 73.3g, **fat** 12.5g, **saturated fat** 7.2g, **fibre** 0.6g, **salt** 0.5g

Sloe gin layer cake

1 hour, plus cooling | serves 12 | easy

200g butter, at room
temperature, plus extra
for greasing
200g golden caster sugar
4 eggs
175g plain flour
1 tsp baking powder
90g ground almonds
100ml buttermilk
4 tbsp flaked almonds

For the filling
100g butter, softened
140g icing sugar, plus more
for dusting
3–4 dark purple plums
150ml sloe gin
30g golden caster sugar

The best use of sloe gin: team with plums and make a layer cake with a wow factor. It's sure to impress your friends and family, and best of all it's an easy recipe too.

Heat the oven to 170°C/Fan 150°C/Gas 3. Cream the butter and sugar together until light and fluffy, then beat in the eggs one by one, adding a tablespoon of flour after the first egg. Fold in the flour, baking powder and ground almonds followed by the buttermilk.

Spoon the mixture into two greased and lined 18cm loose-based cake tins and sprinkle the almonds over the surface of each tin. Bake for 30–35 minutes, or until the cakes are risen and golden. Cool on wire racks.

Meanwhile, beat the butter for the filling until it's light and creamy and beat in the icing sugar to make a buttercream.

Tip the plums into a pan with the sloe gin and sugar and cook them together until the plums just soften but hold their shape. Scoop out and cool the plums. Reduce the liquid to a syrup.

Sandwich the cakes together with some of the syrup and the buttercream. Decorate with the plums, a few flaked almonds and a drizzle of the syrup.

Per serving 494 kcals, **protein** 7.4g, **carbohydrate** 43.7g, **fat** 29.7g, **saturated fat** 14.2g, **fibre** 1.4g, **salt** 0.6g

Pistachio and chocolate stripe cake

3 hours | serves 10 | tricky but worth it

12 eggs
360g golden caster sugar,
  plus extra for dusting
240g self-raising flour
120g ground pistachios
  (if you are grinding your
  own, look for lovely
  green pistachio slivers
  for the best colour)
120g butter, melted

For the frosting
200g butter
400g icing sugar
200g dark chocolate
200ml double cream

This pistachio and chocolate stripe cake is a delicious combination of flavours and it looks fantastic. It is a little tricky, but completely worth the effort. Make sure you use pistachios with a good, strong colour.

Heat the oven to 180°C/Fan 160°C/Gas 4. Measure the ingredients for the sponge in three batches (4 eggs, 120g sugar, 80g flour, 40g pistachios and 40g butter). Line a 21 x 31cm baking tray or tin with non-stick baking paper. Whisk one batch of eggs and sugar together until they are light and fluffy – this will take about 5 minutes. Fold in the flour and pistachios then the butter. Spoon the mixture into the tin and level it out. Bake for 12 minutes, or until the sponge is springy and cooked through, but still pale in colour.

Leave to cool for 3 minutes and then carefully invert the cake onto another piece of baking paper that has been dusted with caster sugar, peel off the layer of paper, and lay it back down. Roll up the sponge and leave it to cool while rolled up. Repeat with the other two batches of sponge but leave these two to cool flat. Put all the frosting ingredients in a pan and heat gently until you have a shiny, smooth mixture. Leave to cool until it is thicker but still spreadable.

Cut each of the flat sponges in half (exactly down the centre) to make two long strips. Unroll the rolled-up sponge and do the same. Trim any stray edges off the sides but try to keep all the strips the same size. Lay one of the strips that had been rolled up on a piece of baking paper and spread a thin layer of frosting all over it. Lay the other rolled piece on top but 2cm inwards from the short edge, then roll them up, folding the bottom piece up and over the top one to get the roll started. When you have a roll, lay another strip down, frost it and join it edge-to-edge onto the roll where the outside strip ends. Repeat until you have used all the strips, then upend the roll onto a cake board and make sure the top is flat – trim it if you need to. Warm the frosting a little until it is shiny and soft enough to spread easily, then frost the outside of the cake. Serve in wedges.

Per serving 1,000 kcals, **protein** 14.4g, **carbohydrate** 102.8g, **fat** 58g, **saturated fat** 30.8g, **fibre** 4.4g, **salt** 1g

Lemon curd layer cake

1 hour, plus cooling | serves 12 | easy

250g butter, very soft, plus
   extra for greasing
250g golden caster sugar
250g self-raising flour
1 tsp baking powder
4 large eggs
2 lemons, zested
1–2 tsp milk

For the decoration
250g butter, very soft
500g icing sugar
3 lemons, zested
   and juiced
1 jar of lemon curd
crystallised flowers,
   to decorate

A showstopping, lemony sponge cake with a delicious curd icing and beautiful edible crystallised flowers. We have used violets and primroses here but feel free to experiment with others. They can be found online and in most bake shops.

Heat the oven to 180°C/Fan 160°C/Gas 4. Butter and line the bases of three 20cm sandwich tins. Beat the butter, sugar, flour, baking powder, eggs and lemon zest together with beaters until you have a smooth batter. Add enough milk so the mix just drops off a spoon.

Divide the mixture between the tins and bake for 20–25 minutes, swapping the tins around halfway through so that they brown evenly. When they're ready, a skewer poked in should come out clean. Cool on wire racks, top-side up.

Make the icing by beating the soft butter with the icing sugar, lemon zest and juice until light and fluffy. Use two-thirds to fill the cake and top each layer with some lemon curd. Frost the top with the rest of the buttercream and finish with crystallised flowers.

Per serving 724 kcals, **protein** 4.4g, **carbohydrate** 91.2g, **saturated fat** 22.7g, **fibre** 0.9g, **salt** 1.1g

Really decadent chocolate and salted caramel mousse cake

2 hours | serves 16 | tricky but worth it

300ml just-boiled water

75g dark chocolate, broken
into pieces

2 tsp instant coffee

pinch of salt

100g cocoa powder

350ml buttermilk

375g plain flour

2 tsp bicarbonate of soda

½ tsp baking powder

3 eggs

500g light brown soft sugar

175ml vegetable oil

2 tsp vanilla extract

For the salted caramel

175g golden caster sugar

120ml double cream

½ tsp sea salt flakes

120g unsalted butter,
cubed

For the ganache

400ml double cream

3 tbsp light brown soft
sugar

2 tbsp golden syrup

2 tsp vanilla extract

600g dark chocolate, very
finely chopped

40g unsalted butter, cubed

This is a spectacular cake, perfect for a celebration. There are a couple of important things to remember with expensive ingredients at stake: chop the chocolate for the ganache very finely so it melts quickly and stops the ganache from seizing and splitting. Make sure the cakes, the salted caramel, the chocolate mousse filling and chocolate ganache are completely cool before filling and finishing the cake; if anything is still warm you will end up with a sticky mess.

Line the bases and sides of three 19–20cm cake tins with non-stick baking paper. Heat the oven to 160°C/Fan 140°C/Gas 3. To make the cakes, pour the just-boiled water over the chocolate in a heatproof bowl and leave it to melt for a couple of minutes, stirring occasionally until smooth. Stir in the coffee, a pinch of salt, the cocoa and the buttermilk. Sift the flour, bicarbonate of soda and baking powder together into a bowl.

In a separate bowl, whisk the eggs, sugar, oil and vanilla extract together for a few minutes until thick and light. Whisk in the flour mixture, followed by the chocolate mixture. The batter will be quite thin. Divide between the prepared tins and bake for about 40 minutes, until well risen and springy to the touch. Cool in the tins for a few minutes, then turn out and cool on wire racks.

For the caramel, pour the sugar into a heavy-based pan and add a few tablespoons of water. Heat gently, stirring only until the sugar dissolves. Turn the heat up to medium-high and allow the syrup to come to the boil undisturbed. Simmer briskly, swirling the pan occasionally but never stirring, until the caramel turns a rich amber colour. Remove from the heat and carefully stir in the cream and salt, followed by the butter cubes. Cool completely.

To make the ganache, bring 300ml of the cream to the boil in a large saucepan with the sugar and the golden syrup. As soon as the mixture boils, remove it from the heat and stir in the vanilla and chocolate. Stir quickly to melt it and immediately scrape about half into a mixing bowl. Add the butter to the remaining ganache in the saucepan and stir gently until melted. Set aside to cool and firm up at room temperature. Stir occasionally. If it seems too runny to spread, chill in the fridge for 30 minutes.

To make the mousse, use an electric whisk to beat the remaining ganache in the mixing bowl. After about a minute, gradually trickle in the remaining 100ml of cream. Keep whisking; it will take 3–5 minutes to become thick.

Halve the three cakes horizontally and put one bottom half on a serving plate edged with thin strips of baking paper to protect the plate from the icing. Spread the top of this base cake with a thin layer of caramel and a thicker layer of the mousse. Top with another cake disc and repeat the caramel and mousse layers. Carry on in this way until all the caramel, mousse and cake discs have been used, finishing with the sixth cake disc (do not top this with caramel). Make sure the cake is straight, not leaning.

Finish by covering the entire cake with the shiny ganache, piling it on top and using a palette knife to sweep it across and down the sides. Take your time to get a smooth finish. Leave the cake to sit for an hour somewhere cool before serving then serve in thin slices; it's very rich! You can chill the cake but it may lose its shine.

Per serving 849 kcals, **protein** 8.1g, **carbohydrate** 89.8g, **fat** 51.1g, **saturated fat** 25.6g, **fibre** 3.4g, **salt** 0.9g

Gingerbread Bundt cake

1½ hours, plus overnight maturing | cuts into 12 | easy

150g unsalted butter, plus extra for greasing

200g plain flour, plus extra for dusting

100g golden syrup

75g dark treacle

175g dark muscovado sugar

75g dark chocolate, chopped

2 balls of stem ginger, finely chopped

100ml Guinness or stout

½ tsp bicarbonate of soda

1 tsp baking powder

3 tsp ground ginger

1 rounded tsp ground cinnamon

½ tsp ground allspice

½ tsp ground nutmeg

pinch of salt

3 medium eggs, beaten

For the glaze

3 tbsp ginger preserve, sieved, or apricot jam

juice of 1 lemon

150g icing sugar, sifted

Guinness and dark chocolate add an extra depth of flavour and slight smokiness to this dark gingerbread. It's best to make in advance and leave uniced in an airtight box overnight and glaze an hour or so before serving. That way the flavours get a chance to really develop.

Heat the oven to 160°C/Fan 140°C/Gas 3. Grease the inside of a 2-litre Bundt tin and lightly dust with plain flour, tipping out the excess.

Put the butter, golden syrup, treacle, sugar and chocolate into a pan. Heat to melt the butter and chocolate and dissolve the sugar. Add the stem ginger and Guinness and heat until hot but not boiling, mixing well. Take off the heat, whisk in the bicarb (it will foam), and leave to cool slightly.

Sift the flour, baking powder and spices with a pinch of salt into a large bowl. Whisk the eggs and the cooled golden syrup mixture into the dry ingredients in three batches, mixing well until completely smooth. Pour the batter into the prepared tin then tap it on the work surface to release any large air bubbles and bake for about 45–50 minutes or until well risen and a wooden skewer inserted into the middle comes out clean.

Remove the cake from the oven and leave it to rest in the tin for no more than 2 minutes, then turn out onto a cooling rack and cool completely. Wrap the cold cake in cling film and leave overnight or for a couple of days before glazing to allow the spice flavours to develop.

To glaze, heat the oven to 160°C/Fan 140°C/Gas 3 and transfer the cake to a baking sheet lined with non-stick baking paper. Warm the ginger preserve, or apricot jam, in a small pan and brush it over the surface of the cake. Pour the lemon juice into a small pan and heat gently until just boiling. Add the icing sugar and stir until melted and smooth.

Leave the lemon icing to cool for 2–3 minutes then brush it all over the surface of the cake in an even layer. Put it back into the oven for 5 minutes until the glaze has become translucent. Let the icing set before serving.

Per serving 364 kcals, **protein** 4g, **carbohydrate** 57g, **fat** 13g, **saturated fat** 8g, **fibre** 0.7g, **salt** 0.4g

Redcurrant and lemon Bundt cake

1 hour 30 minutes, plus cooling | serves 12 | easy

200g butter
500g golden caster sugar
60ml flavourless oil
zest of 2 lemons
4 eggs
350g plain flour
1 tbsp baking powder
250ml buttermilk
200g redcurrants, removed
   from their stems

For the decoration
200g icing sugar
juice of 2 lemons
   (optional)

This beautiful cake is made in a Heritage Bundt tin. It isn't cheap but it will last forever and works like a dream – the cakes release perfectly every time. You can, of course, use another ring-shaped tin.

Heat the oven to 180°C/Fan 160°C/Gas 4. Beat the butter, sugar and oil in a stand mixer until the mixture looks light and fluffy. Beat in the lemon zest, followed by the eggs.

Sift the flour and baking powder together. Fold this into the cake mix, adding the buttermilk as you do so. Fold until the mixture is smooth. Fold through the redcurrants. Spoon into a buttered and floured Bundt tin or cake tin.

Bake for 1 hour, then check that the sides of the cake are starting to shrink away from the edges and the top is pale brown. Cool in the tin for a few minutes, then turn out onto a wire rack.

To decorate, either dust heavily with icing sugar or mix enough lemon juice with the icing sugar to make a glaze and brush it all over the cake.

Per serving 536 kcals, **protein** 6g, **carbohydrate** 80.2g, **fat** 21g, **saturated fat** 9.7g, **fibre** 2g, **salt** 0.7g

Rum and raisin Bundt

1 hour 45 minutes, plus overnight soaking and cooling | cuts into 15 slices | easy

350g raisins

100ml dark rum

225g butter, softened, plus extra for greasing

175g light muscovado sugar

4 medium eggs

350g plain flour, plus extra for dusting

7g sachet of fast-action or easy-bake yeast

1 tbsp baking powder

2 tsp vanilla extract

50ml milk

pinch of salt

For the glaze

100g light muscovado sugar

50g butter

3 tbsp dark rum

Rum and raisin is a real crowd-pleasing flavour combo. Try this warm, for pudding, dolloped with sweetened whipped cream.

The night before you want to make the cake, mix the raisins and rum together and leave them to soak overnight (stirring a couple of times, if you remember).

The next day, drain the raisins reserving any leftover rum. Put 200g of the raisins and the rum in a food processor with the butter and sugar, and whizz until really smooth. Add the eggs, flour, yeast, baking powder, vanilla and milk with a pinch of salt and whizz again. Scrape the mixture into a mixing bowl, cover with cling film and leave at room temperature to rise for an hour.

Heat the oven to 170°C/Fan 150°C/Gas 3½ and grease and lightly flour a large Bundt tin (approximately 23cm). Fold the rest of the raisins through the batter, then spoon the mix into the tin and smooth the top. Bake for 50–60 minutes or until a skewer poked into the thickest part of the cake comes out clean. Turn out onto a wire rack to cool.

Put the glaze ingredients in a pan and heat gently until the sugar has dissolved, then bubble together for a few minutes until shiny and saucy. Cool until it starts to thicken, then pour over the cake to glaze. Cool until set. Cut the cake into generous wedges.

Per serving 407 kcals, **protein** 5g, **carbohydrate** 51.6g, **fat** 17g, **saturated fat** 10.1g, **fibre** 1.6g, **salt** 0.6g

Chocolate gâteau with raspberry, rose and vanilla cream

1½ hours, plus cooling | serves 12 | easy

250g butter, plus extra for
  greasing
125g plain flour
125g self-raising flour
50g good-quality cocoa
  powder
½ tsp baking powder
350g golden caster sugar
150g light muscovado
  sugar
100g 36% milk chocolate
150g 72% dark chocolate
180ml water
125ml milk
4 eggs

**For the rose filling
and topping**
200ml double cream
100g icing sugar
a few drops of rose water
a few drops of pink
  colouring
4 tbsp raspberry jam
200g fresh raspberries
icing sugar, for dusting
crystallised rose petals,
  to decorate

**A wonderfully moist chocolate cake that is easy to make. The touch
of fruit and cream makes it lighter than most and perfect for any
time of year.**

Heat the oven to 160°C/Fan 140°C/Gas 3. Grease and line three 18cm
sandwich tins with non-stick baking paper (this is a runny batter, so if
your tins have loose bases, make sure they fit tightly).

Sift the flours, cocoa and baking powder into a bowl and stir in the sugars.
Melt the chocolates together with the water and butter in a pan. Beat the
milk with the eggs. Add the chocolate mixture and egg mixture to the flour
and whisk well until there are no lumps. Divide the mixture between the
tins and bake for 40–50 minutes or until risen and firm to the touch. Cool
on wire racks in the tins for 30 minutes and then turn out to finish cooling.

Beat the cream to soft peaks and then beat in 2 tablespoons of icing sugar,
rose water and some pink colouring. Mix the remaining icing sugar with a
little colouring, a drop of rose water and a splash of water, if needed. It
should be runny and quite pink.

Put a layer of cake on a stand, spread with 2 tablespoons of jam and then
spoon on half of the rose cream. Sprinkle over half of the raspberries. Add
another layer of cake and the remaining jam, rose cream and raspberries.
Put on the top layer and dust it with icing sugar.

Run the pink icing around the outside edge of the cake in rings (don't
worry if it forms beads) and use it to stick on the crystallised rose petals.

Per serving 681 kcals, **protein** 7.3g, **carbohydrate** 77.6g, **fat** 37.2g, **saturated fat** 22.2g, **fibre** 3.2g, **salt** 0.7g

Glossy chocolate cherry cake

1 hour, plus cooling | serves 12 | a little effort

250g plain flour
60g 70% cocoa powder
1 tsp bicarbonate of soda
1 tsp baking powder
200g caster sugar
200g soft dark brown sugar
2 eggs, beaten
125ml buttermilk
1 tsp vanilla extract
1 tbsp chocolate extract
 (you'll find this in the
 baking section) or brandy
125g unsalted butter,
 cubed
1 tsp salt
240ml water
350g jar of pitted morello
 cherries, drained

For the shiny ganache
250ml double cream
3 tbsp golden syrup
250g 70% dark chocolate,
 finely chopped
1 tsp vanilla extract
crème fraîche or whipped
 cream, to serve

This is a feather-light, divinely squidgy chocolate cake studded with cherries and iced with a shiny ganache.

Heat the oven to 190°C/Fan 170°C/Gas 5. Line a 20 x 30cm tin with non-stick baking paper. Sift the flour, cocoa, bicarbonate of soda and baking powder into a large mixing bowl. Stir in the sugars, mixing everything together. In a separate bowl, whisk the eggs, buttermilk, vanilla and chocolate extracts or brandy together briefly.

Put the butter and salt in a saucepan with the water and set the pan over a medium heat, then remove the pan as soon as the water boils. Pour this into the dry mixture and begin to stir it in with a spatula or big metal spoon. Next, pour in the egg mixture and fold together well.

Scatter the cherries over the base of the tin and spoon the batter over. Bake for 25–30 minutes, or until risen and springy. Carefully turn out the cake, peeling away the paper, then turn onto a wire rack the right way up to cool.

To make the ganache, bring the cream and syrup almost to the boil in a small pan. Put the chopped chocolate in a heat proof bowl with the vanilla extract and pour the hot cream over the top. Leave for a minute, then gently stir to form a glossy ganache. Spread over the top and sides of the cooled cake, smoothing with a palette knife. Serve with crème fraîche or cream on the side.

Per serving 575 kcals, **protein** 5.9g, **carbohydrate** 71.2g, **fat** 31.4g, **saturated fat** 17g, **fibre** 2.6g, **salt** 0.8g

Raspberry red velvet angel cake

2 hours, plus cooling | makes 10 slices | easy

175g golden caster sugar

75g plain flour

50g cocoa powder

200g raspberries, plus extra
to serve

6 large egg whites

½ tsp cream of tartar

1 tsp vanilla extract

pinch of salt

artificial red food colouring
(natural versions lose
their colour when baked)

For the icing

225g golden caster sugar

¼ tsp cream of tartar

1 tsp vanilla extract

2 egg whites

This is a mash-up of two classic American cakes. Don't be tempted to butter the tin – an angel cake needs a grease-free surface to cling on to as it rises and you should lose a very thin outer layer of the crust when you remove the cake from the tin. You'll need a 20–22cm angel cake or savarin tin for this recipe.

Heat the oven to 160°C/Fan 140°C/Gas 3. Mix 75g of the sugar with the flour and cocoa. Whizz the raspberries to a smooth purée in a food processor.

Beat the egg whites to soft peaks in a clean bowl, then add the cream of tartar, vanilla and a good pinch of salt. Beat in the remaining sugar in three additions – each time beating the mixture back to soft peaks before adding more sugar. Beat in some food colouring to make a pale raspberry colour. Sift over half of the flour-cocoa mixture, and gently fold in with a large spatula. Repeat to fold in the rest, then gently fold in the raspberry purée.

Scrape the mixture into a 20–22cm round and about 8–10cm deep ring or savarin tin. Tap the tin once, sharply, on the kitchen surface to remove any air bubbles, then smooth the top and bake for 45 minutes. Invert the tin onto a cooling rack and cool for 1 hour before using a palette knife to help you remove the cake from the tin to allow it to cool completely. You'll need to do a bit of gentle prising but it will come away eventually and any imperfections will be hidden by the frosting.

To make the icing, gently heat the sugar, tartar and vanilla with a few tablespoons of water in a small pan until the sugar has dissolved. Beat the egg whites to soft peaks in a mixing bowl. Bring the sugar mixture to a simmer, then with your electric whisk running, gradually add it to the egg whites and continue beating for 5–10 minutes until stiff peaks form. Swirl the frosting all over the cake and serve with some extra raspberries.

Per serving 169 kcal, **protein** 3.9g, **carbohydrate** 35.6g, **fat** 1.2g, **saturated fat** 0.7g, **fibre** 0.7g, **salt** 0.3g

Ginger and orange Christmas cake

5 hours, plus soaking and cooling | serves 12 | a little effort

600g currants, sultanas and
 raisins
100g glacé cherries
50g mixed peel
50g glacé ginger, roughly
 chopped
100g glacé or diced
 pineapple, roughly
 chopped
60ml Cointreau or Grand
 Marnier
60ml ginger wine
2 tbsp Angostura bitters
225g light muscovado sugar
250g butter, softened
225g plain flour
1 tsp ground ginger
¼ nutmeg, grated
1 tsp ground cinnamon
1 tbsp vanilla extract
100g blanched almonds
4 eggs
zest of 1 orange

For the decoration
2 tbsp apricot jam, mixed
 with 1 tbsp water
500g marzipan
cornflour, for dusting
4 tbsp vodka
500g ready to roll
 fondant icing

This is just the recipe if you would like to try something new for your holiday pud. Fill any holes and dips in the cake with extra marzipan before you cover it with the marzipan layer.

Soak all the dried and glacé fruit in the alcohol and Angostura bitters for up to two days.

Heat the oven to 140°C/Fan 120°C/Gas 1. Line an 18cm square or 20cm round cake tin with two layers of non-stick baking paper.

Beat the sugar and butter together then sift in the flour and spices and mix briefly. Add the vanilla, almonds, eggs, orange zest and the fruit and alcohol mix and stir together. Spoon the mixture into the tin and make a dip in the centre with the back of a spoon so that when the cake rises in the middle you get a flat top. Bake for 3–3½ hours then turn off the oven and leave to cool in the tin in the oven.

Remove the cake from the tin, peel off the paper and brush off any crumbs, then brush the top of the cake with sieved jam. Roll out the marzipan on a work surface dusted with cornflour until it is big enough to cover the cake. Lift it over the cake using a rolling pin and smooth it down all the way around. Trim any excess. Brush with vodka, then roll out the icing and cover the cake in the same way. Trim the icing around the edges and neaten. Roll out the icing off-cuts and cut out different sized stars, brush with a little vodka and stick them to the cake. Serve in large squares.

Per serving 924 kcals, **protein** 10.5g, **carbohydrate** 156.2g, **fat** 29.9g, **saturated fat** 12.4g, **fibre** 3.4g, **salt** 0.57g

Index

Photography credits

BISCUITS AND TRAY BAKES
Double-dipped peanut biscuits SAM STOWELL
Pistachio and fig cookies LARA HOLMES
Soft-baked white chocolate macadamia cookies GUS FILGATE
Cobnut and chocolate shortbreads PHILIP WEBB
Black and white pinwheel cookies JEAN CAZALS
Chocolate cherry cookies GARETH MORGANS
Pistachio and passion fruit yo-yos DAVID MUNNS
Chocolate and jasmine tea kisses GARETH MORGANS
Blackberry ripple ice cream sandwiches GARETH MORGANS
Raspberry and lemon flapjacks ANT DUNCAN
Toasted almond and caramel millionaires' shortbread GARETH MORGANS
Nut and oat breakfast bars ANT DUNCAN

TARTS AND PASTRIES
Pear and hazelnut Bakewell STUART OVENDEN
Double chocolate brownie tart with boozy cream MYLES NEW
Jelly and custard cream slice STUART OVENDEN
Raspberry lime curd tart GUS FILGATE
Espresso tart with hazelnut pastry STUART OVENDEN
Pecan, maple and bourbon tart LARA HOLMES
Apple and cheddar crust pie STUART OVENDEN
Pumpkin pie with maple cream PHILIP WEBB
Lemon meringue pies GUS FILGATE
Rose and almond choux buns STUART OVENDEN
Gooseberry sugar-crust pie PHILIP WEBB
Little Linzer tarts GARETH MORGANS
Panna cotta tart with roasted plums LARA HOLMES
Peach Melba tart PETER CASSIDY
Cherry blondie tart PHILIP WEBB
Passion fruit tart with meringue PHILIP WEBB
Lemon curd and blackberry tart MYLES NEW
Dark chocolate and salted caramel tart JEAN CAZALS

MINI TREATS
Cinnamon buns LARA HOLMES
Mini jam doughnuts GARETH MORGANS
Apple and raspberry breakfast muffins GARETH MORGANS
Pear, saffron and browned butter muffins GARETH MORGANS
Banana and almond butter muffins ANT DUNCAN
Pumpkin pie spiced muffins ANT DUNCAN
Blueberry crumble cakes GUS FILGATE
Ginger madeleines SIMON WALTON
Cappuccino eclairs MYLES NEW
Butterscotch bars with toffee cream GARETH MORGANS
Raspberry and white chocolate blondies GIS FILGATE
Black forest brownies ANT DUNCAN
Sticky toffee squares SAM STOWELL
Mint choc chip brownies MAJA SMEND
Peanut butter and caramel brownies LARA HOLMES
Rosemary and demerara shortbread SIAN IRVINE
Pistachio fancies DAVID MUNN
Fresh cherry and coconut lamingtons STUART OVENDEN
Raspberry and white chocolate macaroons GUS FILGATE
Black forest cupcakes GARETH MORGANS

Blackberry and chocolate cakes GARETH MORGANS
Lemon and blueberry cupcakes LARA HOLMES
Coffee and walnut cupcakes ANT DUNCAN
Party cupcakes SIAN IRVINE
Sour cherry cakes with cream cheese frosting ANT DUNCAN

CAKES FOR PUDDING
Amalfi lemon drizzle cake ANT DUNCAN
Strawberry and Earl Grey roulade STUART OVENDEN
Banana loaf with passion fruit frosting SAM STOWELL
Orange and dark chocolate cake LARA HOLMES
Cherry Bakewell tart PETER CASSIDY
Caramel chip banana cake MAJA SMEND
Coconut loaf with lime and lemon drizzle GARETH MORGANS
Earl Grey tea loaf ADRIAN LAWRENCE
Coffee and walnut Swiss roll MAJA SMEND
Double chocolate and raspberry babka SAM STOWELL
Mississippi mud pie PHILIP WEBB
Carrot cake with maple frosting ANT DUNCAN
Easiest-ever chocolate fudge cake GARETH MORGANS
Lemon polenta cake MYLES NEW
Orange, almond and olive oil cake LARA HOLMES
White chocolate and raspberry cheesecake DAVID MUNNS
Passion fruit layer cake PHILIP WEBB
Chocolate and almond cake GARETH MORGANS
Simple sponge GARETH MORGANS
Texas sheet cake GARETH MORGANS
Strawberry and pistachio cake PHILIP WEBB
Plum and almond sheet cake PHILIP WEBB

SHOW-OFF CAKES
Strawberry eclairs PHILIP WEBB
Strawberry dream ANT DUNCAN
Pistachio and chocolate roulade GARETH MORGANS
Lemon and white chocolate layer loaf SAM STOWELL
Rhubarb Bakewell ADRIAN LAWRENCE
Upside-down apple and star anise cake STUART OVENDEN
Chocolate tiramisu torte DEBI TRELOAR
Fluffy coconut and lime cake SIMON WALTON
Roman cheesecake GARETH MORGANS
White chocolate fudge cake ANT DUNCAN
Devil's food cake with orange frosting SAM STOWELL
Vanilla, chocolate and caramel layer cake GARETH MORGANS
Grapefruit and poppy seed angel cake GARETH MORGANS
Sloe gin layer cake PHILIP WEBB
Pistachio and chocolate stripe cake SAM STOWELL
Lemon curd layer cake DAVID MUNNS
Really decadent chocolate and salted caramel mousse cake LARA HOLMES
Gingerbread Bundt cake GARETH MORGANS
Redcurrant and lemon Bundt cake GARETH MORGANS
Rum and raisin Bundt GARETH MORGANS
Chocolate gateau with raspberry rose and vanilla cream GARETH MORGANS
Glossy chocolate cherry cake GUS FILGATE
Raspberry and red velvet angel cake STUART OVENDEN
Ginger and orange Christmas cake BRETT STEVENS